ENDORSEMENTS

Heather Zempel is one of God's great gifts to today's church. Her wisdom and insight on leading small groups, opening up the Scripture in fresh ways, and helping people discover new depths of God are breathtaking. This is a book you can't afford to miss.

> —**Margaret Feinberg**, author of *Wonderstruck* and *Scouting the Divine*

Heather ventures where most pastors fear to tread, grinding through the gritty pages of a neglected prophet who's been waiting for someone courageous enough to tell his story. Raw truth, relentless love, and enduring passion fill these pages. Prepare to be amazed!

> —**Dr. Bill Donahue**, best-selling author and professor, Trinity International University

Heather reveals her passion for stirring up the next generation's love for the Bible as she tackles the book of Habakkuk head on. That's right, Habakkuk! An emerging voice in the church, Heather is always willing to get into the mess of the difficult areas of Scripture. She asks hard-hitting questions about life and faith and pain, but she does so with compassion, grace, and a healthy dose of humor. To find strength for the journey, read this book.

> —**Christine Caine**, Founder, the A21 Campaign and best-selling author, *Undaunted*

When Heather Zempel speaks, I listen. She has a prophetic voice that will challenge your assumptions, helping you see God and yourself in new ways. She doesn't tapdance around the truth. She grapples with it in a way that is transforming.

> —**Mark Batterson**, *New York Times* best-selling author and lead pastor of National Community Church

Are you brave enough to ask the tough questions—especially the tough questions about faith? That's what I love about Heather Zempel. She's not afraid to ask the questions the rest of us are thinking but are unwilling to voice. In *Amazed and Confused* Heather boldly confronts our questions and yet gently reminds us that God is love. Whether on your own or with a group, you need to allow yourself to take this journey where your faith will be both amazed and confused.

> —**Jenni Catron**, church leader and author of
> *Clout: Discover and Unleash Your God-Given Influence*

With the intellectual capacity of a theologian, and a social worker's sensitivity to the abilities of the rest of us, Heather unearths the gospel through the story of Habakkuk. You will laugh, cry, and intimately engage with the true God, not just the God you have created in your own mind.

> —**Rick Howerton**, Small Group and Discipleship Specialist, LifeWay Church Resources; author of *Destination Community: Small Group Ministry Manual* and *A Different Kind of Tribe: Embracing the New Small Group Dynamic*

AMAZED
and
CONFUSED

When God's Actions Collide With Our Expectations

• ◦ ☺ ◦ •

HEATHER ZEMPEL

THOMAS NELSON
Since 1798

NASHVILLE   DALLAS   MEXICO CITY   RIO DE JANEIRO

Published in Nashville, Tennessee, by Thomas Nelson. Thomas Nelson is a trademark of HarperCollins Christian Publishing, Inc.

Thomas Nelson titles may be purchased in bulk for educational, business, fund-raising, or sales promotional use. For information, please e-mail SpecialMarkets@ThomasNelson.com.

Page design and layout: Crosslin Creative
Feather image: vectorstock.com

ISBN: 9781401679231

Printed in the United States of America

14 15 16 17 18 19 RRD 6 5 4 3 2 1

To my teachers at Cottage Hill Baptist School for instilling in me an insatiable hunger for the Word of God.

ACKNOWLEDGMENTS

To Ryan Zempel, who puts up with me when I'm amazing and when I'm confusing.

To my Sawyer family and Zempel family for loving me and believing in me.

To Mark and Lora Batterson and National Community Church for encouraging me to write and letting me talk about Habakkuk all the time.

To all those who amaze me with their overwhelming prayer and support—Margaret Feinberg and Leif Oines for consistently pushing me; Dave Buehring and Heidi Scanlon for praying this book into existence; the Gang, Team D, Discipleship Journey girls and the Hungry Mothers for their constant friendship.

To Maegan Hawley for loving the Minor Prophets as much as I do and encouraging me to help others love them too. To Jenilee Hurley for loving life in all its confusion and amazement as much as I do. To Emily Hendrickson for wearing out her eyes reading drafts, wearing out her ears listening to ideas, and wearing out her knees in prayer during the writing process, and for consuming copious amounts of chocolate croissants with me.

To Mike, Aaron, Gregg, Christy, Leslie, and the Hendrickson family for trusting God in impossible circumstances so that His faithfulness could be put on display.

To Frank, Maleah, Jennifer, Bethany, my fellow Inscribed authors, and my Thomas Nelson family for believing that God is both amazing and confusing and for making this book a reality.

CONTENTS

INTRODUCTION

GOD IS . . .

God is not nice.

I've searched the Scriptures forwards, backwards, and sideways in various translations, and I've yet to find one place where Scripture declares that God is nice. In fact, there are plenty of moments when God seems to act in ways that are anything *but* nice. He floods the earth, kills Egyptian babies, and makes Hosea marry a prostitute. And it's not as though things lighten up at all when Jesus shows up. He tells a guy he can't go bury his parents before becoming a disciple, declares that a Syro-Phoenician woman is not worthy of his assistance, and calls the Pharisees "whitewashed tombs" (Matt. 23:27 NKJV). That's ancient smack talk for "You look good on the outside, but inside you smell like death."

God doesn't claim to be nice. He claims to be love, and there is a big difference. Our problem is that when we read, "God is love," sometimes those words get translated from the page to our cerebral cortexes as "God is nice." We expect and settle for a God who is well mannered and plays well with others instead of daring to embrace the wild, ferocious, and jealous God of love. If we fail to make the distinction between "God is nice" and "God is love," we will also fail to grasp the beauty of the gospel, and we will misunderstand or ignore many passages of Scripture that reveal something important about the glory of God.

It's an incomplete understanding of God's love that prompts us to say things like, "My God would never . . ." or "I just don't believe a loving God would allow bad things to happen to good people," or "If God is loving, how can He send people to hell?" Our finite ability to comprehend God's infinite love limits our capacity for reconciling what we believe to be true about God's character with the problems of evil and pain we see in the world around us. When we come to those chapters of ache, confusion, suffering, and disorientation in our lives, we often follow a path that either ignores God or ignores the problem. We close our eyes, shut out the pain, and skim through those thorny chapters as quickly as we skim through those same kinds of chapters in Scripture. Or we respond with pithy and hollow statements of saccharine spirituality—"God must have His reasons," "One day we will be thankful," "I guess heaven just needed another angel," and other empty sentiments.

Part of the problem with understanding God's character in the midst of our disordered world is that we fail to read and embrace the *whole* story of Scripture. Instead of reading the Bible as the actual history of real, messed-up people who lived in the same messed-up world we live in, we approach it as if it is a fairy tale, with perfect heroes and perfectly rotten villains who live in a world where the good guys always win and the bad guys always lose. We only remember and teach certain parts of the story. For instance . . .

- Noah saved the earth—we forget he was later found drunk and naked in his tent.

- Jonah obeyed God—we neglect to mention that he also whined and demanded a judgment-day fireworks show.

- Samson saved Israel by knocking down the Philistine temple—but we forget *why* he was in the temple in the first place: because he was enslaved after bedding Delilah and giving away proprietary information during pillow talk.

Additionally, we often only teach and remember some scripture verses outside the context of their larger story. Take, for example, Philippians 4:13, a verse we memorize to motivate ourselves. It reads, "I can do all things through Christ who strengthens me" (NKJV). The implication is that we can succeed at whatever we want because we are on Jesus' team; however, if we look at the original context, we see that Paul was referring to his ability to live and thrive in whatever circumstances life threw into his path. Instead of appealing to Jesus' power to make him successful, Paul was declaring the strength God gave him to weather any situation—whether storm or fair weather, times of abundance or time of need, in sickness and in health. We may do better to memorize it in The Voice translation: "I can be content in any and every situation through the Anointed One who is my power and strength."

Toward the end of the Old Testament lurks the message of an obscure prophet by the name of Habakkuk. His writings have sparked major growth spurts in the history of the church, but they've also at times been misunderstood and misappropriated to paint a false picture of God's niceness when, in reality, his message is more textured, layered, and difficult to bear.

For instance, God told Habakkuk to "write down the revelation and make it plain on tablets so that a herald may run with it" (Hab. 2:2 NIV). This verse often becomes the foundational text for New Year's sermons on goal setting and following our God-given dreams. Unfortunately, when we read a little bit more, we discover that the revelation God was referring to involved lots of death and destruction . . . of the good guys.

We also find this gem in the book of Habakkuk: "Look at the nations and watch—and be utterly amazed. For I am going to do something in your days that you would not believe, even if you were told" (1:5 NIV). This passage easily becomes the text for sermons and studies on all the great things God is going to do for us. We are going to be amazed! But if we keep reading, we discover that the aforementioned death and destruction of the good guys will be executed by the Babylonians—the bad guys. Amazed? Yes. But in a way that leaves us completely confused.

Habakkuk's God is not one who promises safety from the agonies of life; rather, He is a God who is sovereign over the agonies of life. Habakkuk's God does not promise deliverance in the valley of the shadow of death, but presence. He is a God of love more extravagant and resolute than we can imagine.

Habakkuk was a man who recognized that God is not always nice, but He is love. This mysterious and oft-forgotten prophet in the little-used pages of our Bibles wrestled with the same questions, uncertainties, and disappointments that we face in our own lives in the modern world. His story can guide us and his relationship with God can inspire us to hold on to faith when it seems faith has let go of us. Before we dig deeper, let's back up to capture even greater perspective.

CHAPTER ONE

THE STORY

"In the beginning, God . . ." (Gen. 1:1). He references Himself more than thirty-five times in the opening chapter of Genesis alone, as if to settle once and for all that He is both the author and the protagonist of this great story.

In the beginning, God created . . . and when He created, light beamed from the heavens and waters covered the earth. Valleys dug deep and mountains sprang high. Birds flew in the air and fish swam in the seas. Insects filled the ground and dinosaurs thundered across the land. The Creator declared that it was good.

Surrounded by four rivers, a garden was planted. In that garden He created a man and a woman, marked in His image—their Storyteller and Creator. God was present, community was perfect, and their life objective was to enjoy relationship with God and one another.

He gave them food to eat . . .

The Lord God made all sorts of trees grow up from the ground—trees that were beautiful and that produced delicious fruit. In the middle of the garden He placed the Tree of Life and the Tree of Knowledge of Good and Evil.

The two trees. The tree that represented the objective: life—breathed by God, eternal, and resulting in perfect communion and wholeness. And the tree that represented the obstacle: the knowledge of good and evil.

Every character in every great story makes a choice. Sometimes even the best characters with the best intentions confuse the obstacle and the objective.

The villain—the thief of the souls of men—crawled into the garden in the form of a serpent and planted a seed of doubt in the woman's heart: "Did God really say . . . ?" (Gen. 3:1 NIV). Embracing the wrong tree, the man and woman reached for the very thing that snatched away the life for

> God is both the author and the protagonist of this great story.

which they were created. They left the Story of God to pursue a story of their own making. And in an act of great grace, God banished them from the garden—protecting them from the Tree of Life. For if they were to eat of that tree, they would be doomed to live forever in a state of brokenness, severed from relationship with their Creator.

The garden would be hidden and the Tree of Life removed from their midst, but God hinted that redemption was already in the works—that the woman's offspring would crush the serpent's head. Distant glimpses of the Messiah. The Story was not over . . . it had just begun.

But the people did not look to God; instead, they spiraled downward more and more into their own evil desires. In a rage of grace, a moment where God's wrath and mercy showed up simultaneously with equal parts intensity of force and love, God decided to begin anew and flooded His creation. He appointed one man, Noah, to build a boat and save humanity through the waters. The rainbow in the sky indicated God's presence and promise for a new story.

But they did not learn; they continued to follow stories that were not true, that did not lead to life, that were not written by the great Author.

Nonetheless, God continued to write His Story. He appeared to a man named Abram and promised that he would become a great nation and that all other nations throughout history would be blessed through him. The age of the patriarchs began. From Abraham to Isaac to Jacob . . . from the miraculous provisions of a ram in the thicket to a night of wrestling with God . . . God remained faithful and promised to these faulty yet faithful men that they were the beginning of a great nation and a new story. The twelve sons of Jacob became the twelve tribes of Israel.

Four hundred years later, God's people found themselves enslaved in a foreign land. God raised up a leader named Moses to lead His people out of slavery and oppression and toward the land He had promised their ancestors centuries before. This was a foreshadowing of the redemptive work of the Messiah. He gave Exodus, Leviticus, and Numbers to record the Law—a pathway to righteousness and relationship with the Storyteller. But they turned away from the Author, longing instead for Egypt, so they were doomed to wander in the wilderness.

Forty years later, a new generation had grown up, and Moses wrote the book of Deuteronomy—a retelling of God's Story, which was their story—to remind them of who they were, whose they were, where they were going, why they were going there, and how they were to live once they arrived.

Led by Joshua, the people of God entered the promised land.

With the people newly settled in the land that was promised them, the era of the judges began. Righteous men and women, appointed by God, provided leadership and counsel. But over and over again, a "generation grew up who did not acknowledge the LORD or remember the mighty things he had done for Israel" (Judg. 2:10 NLT).

They forgot the Story.

Looking around, the people desired to be like the other great nations they saw. They did not trust the sovereignty or the grace of their Storyteller and sought to establish leadership they could *see* . . . they asked for a king—and God gave them what they asked for (1 Sam. 8–9).

As time passed, Saul showed the weakness of a king, David showed the redemption of a king, and Solomon showed the danger of a king who takes his eye off the giver of wisdom. At the end of Solomon's reign, the pride of men caused a great rift in the palace, and the great kingdom split in two. The ten tribes of the north strayed from the line of David, built new places of worship, and became known as Israel. A series of evil and corrupted kings sat on its throne.

The two tribes of the south remained centered at Jerusalem, embraced the line of David, and became known as Judah. Some of its kings were generous and kind and turned their hearts toward God. Other kings were seduced by the stories of other gods. Some were a tragic mix of good and evil.

For two centuries God's people existed as two separate nations—sometimes at peace, sometimes at war.

> The people of God did not trust the sovereignty or grace of their Storyteller and sought to establish leadership they could *see*.

The prophets thundered warnings—reminding the people of their Story, of their Maker, and pleading with them to return to the Story where they belonged.

But the people did not listen.

In 722 BC, the Assyrians conquered the Northern Kingdom of Israel and scattered God's people across their empire. Thirsty for dominance, they next turned their eyes toward Judah. They marched on Jerusalem and taunted the people of God at the city gates. Under the noble reign of King Hezekiah and the prayerful guidance of the prophet Isaiah, the Assyrians were miraculously defeated outside the gates of Jerusalem. Judah was safe . . . for now . . . and Isaiah wrote of a coming Messiah.

But the time for that chapter of the Story had not yet come. A new empire was rising. The Babylonians, a ruthless, impetuous, and dreaded people, were marching across the earth, leaving destruction and despair in their wake, and their eyes turned toward Judah.

Neglecting worship and forgetting God, the people of Judah were ruled by corrupt and power-hungry kings who believed they were invincible. The prophets wept, for though they knew God was slow to anger, they also recognized He was jealous for His name and His people. Through their cries, they also pointed to the dawning of a new day of hope and salvation. Habakkuk thus stepped into the spotlight on the stage of the Story of God.

THE VOICES

We often think of the Bible as one long, continuous book. In reality, it is a collection of sixty-six books written by approximately forty authors over the course of sixteen hundred years. The Old Testament contains thirty-nine books, written between 1450 and 400 BC, which tell the story of God's pursuit of and relationship with one family who became the Jewish people. The New Testament is made up of twenty-seven books and letters, all written in the first century AD. These tell the story of Jesus of Nazareth, the Savior promised in the Old Testament.

The books were written by myriad voices—fisherman, tax collectors, shepherds, kings, doctors, political prisoners and advisers, farmers, and poets—and the style of each book is as unique as its author—histories, prophecies, poetry, letters, law, and visions of the future. At the same time, the books tell one cohesive and central story about a passionate God on a relentless pursuit to redeem His creation.

In the Old Testament, the books are grouped into categories as follows:

1. THE LAW

Genesis, Exodus, Leviticus, Numbers, Deuteronomy

The primary themes and stories in these books include:

- The primeval stories of the creation, the flood, and the tower of Babel

- The age of the patriarchs (Abraham, Isaac, and Jacob) and God's promises to Israel

- The fall and rise of Joseph and Israel's captivity in Egypt

- The miraculous exodus from Egypt and the engraving of the Ten Commandments

- The design and construction of the tabernacle

- The complete law of Moses

2. HISTORY

Joshua, Judges, Ruth, 1 and 2 Samuel, 1 and 2 Kings, 1 and 2 Chronicles, Ezra, Nehemiah, Esther. These books cover the narrative history of the Old Testament.

The primary themes and stories in these books include:

- The conquest of the promised land

- The era of the judges (Gideon, Samson, Deborah, Samuel, etc.)

- The kings of Israel

- The building of the temple

- The division of the kingdom

- The exile in Babylon and the return to Judah

The remaining books are poetic and prophetic writings that are grouped together at the end but were written at various points throughout the histories.

3. POETRY

Job, Psalms, Proverbs, Ecclesiastes, Song of Songs (or Song of Solomon), Lamentations

Primary themes include:

- Poetry
- Philosophy
- Prayer and praise
- Love songs
- Suffering and survival

4. THE PROPHETS

Isaiah, Jeremiah, Ezekiel, Daniel, Hosea, Joel, Amos, Obadiah, Jonah, Micah, Nahum, Habakkuk, Zephaniah, Haggai, Zechariah, Malachi

Primary themes include:

- Declarations of God's character
- Guidance
- Judgment of sin
- Hope for the future

O. Palmer Robertson explained, "If Moses and Joshua provided the direction for Israel in their possession of the land, then the writing prophets provided the direction for Israel through their loss of land."[1] The exile was ultimately a redemptive act of God, and the prophets gave guidance and hope to help people navigate the tragedy. The major prophets include Isaiah, Jeremiah, Ezekiel, and Daniel. They

> **The exile was ultimately a redemptive act of God, and the prophets gave guidance and hope.**

are referred to as "major" only because their writings are significantly longer than the others, and not because their messages are somehow more important. Gordon Fee explains to us that their designation stems from Latin translations of the Bible that categorized them that way. In Latin, "minor" meant "shorter," not "less important." Conversely, "major" meant "longer," not "more important."[2]

The minor prophets include Hosea, Joel, Amos, Obadiah, Jonah, Micah, Nahum, Habakkuk, Zephaniah, Haggai, Zechariah, and Malachi. Ancient Judaism grouped them together as one long book called "The Twelve." When compiled, the book was longer than Ezekiel and Daniel but shorter than Isaiah and Jeremiah.

Some of the prophets wrote in and to the Northern Kingdom, while others wrote in and to the Southern Kingdom. Later prophets included those who wrote during and after the exile in Babylon.

• ◉ ● READING THE PROPHETS

Several years ago, a friend of mine commented, "I really hope I don't get seated next to Obadiah at the Marriage Supper of the Lamb, because I'm going to have to tell him, 'I'm really sorry, dude, but I never read your book.'"

I laughed, but I also embraced a new mission to help people navigate the odd world of prophetic writings. They seem so weird and irrelevant. In *Handbook on the Prophets*, author and professor Robert Chisholm admits:

> The prophetic literature of the Hebrew Bible presents great interpretive obstacles. Its poetry, though teeming with vivid imagery that engages the imagination and emotions, challenges the reader's understanding because of its economy of expression, rapid shifts in mood, and sometimes cryptic allusions. The reader of the prophetic literature quickly realizes that these books were written at particular points in time to specific groups of people with whom the modern reader seems to share little.[3]

So true. However, Chisholm also contends that they demand our attention because they are the Word of God and contain a message that transcends time and space by helping us see dimensions of God's character more clearly and challenging us to relate to Him and the world around us according to His ways.

As I read the prophets with new eyes, I realized they were more relevant than I had thought. The prophets accepted the tension of living in a fallen world while waiting hopefully for a new world to come. Their hearts pounded for justice, and they warned that religion was empty unless accompanied by action. They lived through circumstances that didn't make sense, questioned authority, and challenged people to live at a level higher than the rest of culture expected of them. To me, it seemed the Prophets might be the most real, raw, and relevant writings in the entire Bible. The world in which these authors lived, though separated from my own by thousands of years and thousands of miles, also felt very

> The Prophets might be the most real, raw, and relevant writings in the entire Bible.

familiar. Their voices and their messages were as critical and germane to my life as they were to a distant generation; it just took some unraveling and cultural and historical insight to ensure their words resonated in my ears the way they hit their original audiences.

Here are some things to keep in mind when reading and interpreting the prophets:

"Prophecy." In the wise and immortal words of Inigo Montoya, "You keep using that word. I do not think it means what you think it means."[4] We tend to think about prophecy as future-oriented. A few clarifications are in order. First, much of biblical prophecy is oriented around *forth*-telling more than *fore*telling. In other words, at its core, prophecy is about declaring the truth of God's character and ways in the midst of earthly realities and providing a new set of lenses through which to view the current circumstances. Second, prophets did not deliver new messages; rather, their words were rooted in the old covenant. The blessings and curses they pronounced were not novel or peculiar to each individual prophet; rather, the prophets echoed the same sentiments declared in Leviticus 26:1–39, Deuteronomy 4:15–40, and Deuteronomy 28:1–46. If you invest some time in reading and studying those passages, your reading of prophetic writing will deliver a richer and more rewarding experience. Finally, in the places where the biblical prophets were obviously foretelling the future, we must bear in mind that it was the future for the original readers but not necessarily the future for us. Less than 2 percent of Old Testament prophecy pertains to the coming Messiah. Less than 5 percent describes the current age. And less than 1 percent concerns *our* future.[5] We need cultural and historical framing in order to fully appreciate their words.

Not only are the prophetic writings different from all the other categories of Scripture, but each prophetic voice reflects a different personality and a unique perspective. Some prophets lived out the message they wanted to convey in dramatic ways. For instance, God told Hosea to marry a prostitute to show His people a picture of His faithfulness to them, and he did. Similarly, He instructed Ezekiel to perform several weird stunts, such as writing words of mourning on a scroll and eating it, baking bread on excrement, and shaving all the hair off his body with a long sword. Ezekiel thus became an ancient performance artist who would have received mixed reviews in an off-off-Broadway experimental lab theater, but his actions were pictures of the prophetic message he carried. While Jonah carried a specific spoken message to the people of Nineveh, the events of his life became a broader message about God's forgiveness and response to repentance.

Other prophets spoke and wrote their messages. While Isaiah, Jeremiah, Amos, and others conveyed various messages of warning, Habakkuk offers us a unique opportunity to eavesdrop on a conversation between God and one of His prophets, and it's particularly interesting because it isn't the

> **The heroic prophet expresses doubts and concerns and dares to question God.**

kind of conversation we might expect: the heroic prophet expresses doubt and concerns and dares to question God.

Habakkuk is a fascinating book because it openly questions the wisdom and actions of God. When the prophet found himself in the midst of circumstances that didn't make sense, he didn't hesitate to throw some questions up in God's face, and he was not afraid to shoot back with raw, unfiltered emotion. He unabashedly gave voice to his doubts, but he was careful to address his doubts *to* God and not *against* God.

Habakkuk was unique from his fellow prophets. Instead of making God's people—the nation of Israel or the nation of Judah—the central characters of his book, the prophet unashamedly positioned God and His character at the center of his writing. While most prophets confronted the people about why they had strayed from God, Habakkuk dared to confront God on why He had seemingly strayed from

His own character. He didn't speak to the people for God; rather, he spoke to God for the people.

Habakkuk is also different in that there is no call for repentance or conditions upon which disaster might be averted. Many of the other prophets contain if-then clauses and conditions. If people repented, be they Ninevites, Israelites, or people of Judah, God would withhold judgment and spare them. Habakkuk doesn't contain an "out"; rather, it directly declares that destruction is imminent.

Robert Chisholm summarizes the dialogue between God and Habakkuk as follows:

HABAKKUK: How long must the unjust triumph? (Habakkuk 1:2–4)

GOD: Justice is on the way! (Habakkuk 1:5–11)

HABAKKUK: You call this justice? (Habakkuk 1:12–2:1)

GOD: Justice will indeed prevail in due time. (Habakkuk 2:2–20)

HABAKKUK: I have heard . . . I will rejoice. (Habakkuk 3:1–19)[6]

• ◦ ● THE TIMES

After the reign of Solomon, the kingdom of Israel passed to his son Rehoboam, who inherited political unrest and constituent discontent. The people requested tax relief and better labor laws. His father's advisers recommended he listen to the people, but his fraternity buddies (or the ancient equivalent thereof) incited him to take revenge for their impudence. He forced the people to work harder, and that didn't increase his approval ratings. A faction of the people followed a former secretary of labor, Jeroboam, in a revolt. In 931, the kingdom of God split in two: the Northern Kingdom of Israel ruled by Jeroboam and the Southern Kingdom of Judah ruled by Rehoboam.

The Northern Kingdom was cut off from the center of religious activity in Jerusalem, so they resorted to idol worship and were led by a series of evil kings. In AD 722, the Assyrian army attacked Israel and besieged its capital city, Samaria, until it fell. Israelites were exiled far away from their homes while foreigners were relocated to Israel to prevent subsequent revolts.

The term "Samaria" can get confusing. Many of us associate the term with those whom the New Testament Jewish people didn't like. Originally, Samaria was a city that served as the capital of the Northern Kingdom. After the Assyrians captured the city, the inhabitants were exported and foreign people were imported, resulting in intermarriage between Jewish and non-Jewish people. By the time of Jesus, Jewish people saw them as half-breeds and unclean.

Under the godly and prayerful leadership of King Hezekiah and his trusted spiritual guide and prophet Isaiah, the Southern Kingdom was spared an attack of the Assyrians. In AD 701, Sennacherib of Assyria attacked cities along the western edge of Judah but was soundly defeated in his siege on Jerusalem when the angel of the Lord killed 185,000 Assyrian soldiers in a single night. The story was so incredible that it was recorded in three different places in Scripture: 2 Kings 18–19, 2 Chronicles 32, and Isaiah 36–39. Judah had been spared . . . for a season.

Habakkuk was a contemporary of the prophets Nahum, Zephaniah, and Jeremiah, which means he lived during the reigns of Josiah (640–609 BC) and Jekoiakim (609–598 BC). King Josiah brought revival to the nation, but when King Jehoiakim rose to the throne, he neglected the godly reforms made by King Josiah and led the nation to political and spiritual ruin. If you are interested in what God thought of King Jehoiakim and how nasty he was, you can read about it in Jeremiah 22:13–19.

Meanwhile, tribes from southern Babylon, called the Chaldeans, were rising in power and defeated the Assyrian army in 612 BC. With the defeat of the Assyrians, the Egyptians invaded Judah and King Josiah was killed in battle. In 605, the Babylonians defeated the Egyptians at Carchemish and began marching on Judah. King Jehoiakim conceded defeat, and Judah became a vassal state. However, Jehoiakim subsequently rebelled, and the Babylonian army marched into Jerusalem in 598–597 BC. The new king, Jehoiachin (keep the names straight, now), surrendered, and the Babylonians crowned Zedekiah the new king. Because of Judah's continuing rebellion, the Babylonians finally invaded and sacked Jerusalem in 586 BC, and the people were sent into exile until the Persians conquered Babylon in 539 BC (still tracking?).

Technically, the Chaldeans were an ethnic group who eventually dominated the region of Babylon. Over time, "Chaldeans" became synonymous with "Babylonians," so different Bible translations use different terms. For the purposes of this study, the terms are used interchangeably.

Nahum spoke to Nineveh in Assyria and declared that God was just, righteous, and loving, and that He would judge the city for its evils. Zephaniah directed his words to the people of Judah, warning them that the "day of the LORD" was coming soon (Zeph. 1:14 NKJV). Jeremiah, often called the weeping prophet, urged the people to return to the Lord before it was too late.

The book of Habakkuk was likely written during the reign of King Jehoiakim, and the prophet's writing reflects his frustration at the king's leadership (Hab. 1:1–4), prophesies the coming Babylonian attacks on Jerusalem (1:5–17), and predicts the eventual defeat of the Babylonians by the Persians (2:1–20). The underlying theme of his book could be summarized, "A matured faith rests humbly but persistently in God's design for establishing righteousness on earth."[7]

In his commentary on Nahum, Habakkuk, and Zephaniah, O. Palmer Robertson recognizes, with significant reservations, an alternative proposal for the dating of the book of Habakkuk. Some have posited that emending Habakkuk

1:6 so that it reads *kittim* (Kittim) rather than *kasdim* (Chaldeans) would date the book around AD 303, and the oppressors would be understood as the Greeks under the rule of Alexander. However, there is no external evidence to support this alternate translation. Additionally, it is worth noting that the Habakkuk *Pesher*—a commentary used by the Jewish sect of Qumran—understood the oppressors to be the Romans of their own time. Robertson underscores, "The fact that the Qumran scribes felt compelled to retain *kasdim* while interpreting its meaning as Kittim would appear to indicate that they had no textual tradition supporting the reading *kittim*."[8] Dating prophecy and interpreting its meaning both locally and universally requires a level of diligence and study. If we commit to engaging in this difficult work, the results can be both rewarding and transformative.

QUESTIONS

1. How does the idea that "God is not nice" strike you? Do you agree or disagree? What is the difference between "God is nice" and "God is love"?

2. Consider a time in your life when God didn't appear to be nice but He proved in the end to be love. How did He reveal His love?

3. Which parts of the Old Testament are you most familiar with? Least familiar with?

4. How might the distinction between "foretelling" and "forth-telling" affect the way you read and understand prophetic books?

5. What are some of the differences between the time we live in and the time of Habakkuk? What are some of the similarities?

6. Read Leviticus 26:1–39; Deuteronomy 4:15–40; and Deuteronomy 28:1–32. What are some of the emerging themes, patterns, and instructions?

7. Read the entire book of Habakkuk in one sitting. Take note of the following:

   a. To whom was Habakkuk talking?

   b. What was Habakkuk talking about?

   c. How did God respond to Habakkuk?

   d. How did Habakkuk respond to God?

   e. Circle all of the names and adjectives that are attributed to God.

   f. Is your primary reaction to the book one of hope or sorrow?

NOTES

CHAPTER TWO

FALLING

This is the vision with which the prophet Habakkuk was burdened.

How long must I cry, O Eternal One,
     and get no answer from You?
Even when I yell to You, "Violence *is all around*!"
     You do nothing to save *those in distress.*
Why do You force me to see these atrocities?
     Why do You make me watch *such* wickedness?
Disaster and violence, conflict and controversy are raging all
     around me.
Your law is powerless *to stop this*; injustice prevails.
     The depraved surround the innocent, and justice is
     perverted. (Hab. 1:1–4)

IN A PIT WITH A BRIEFCASE ON A RAINY DAY

I fell into a hole. A seven-foot sinkhole. I'm known for my clumsiness and inattentiveness, so counting up the number of times that I stumble or fall is a favorite pastime of my friends. But this time was different. There was no preexisting hole that I inadvertently walked into. The ground literally opened up and swallowed me.

In the fall of 2004, I worked full-time in the U.S. Senate as an advisor on environment and energy policy while also serving part-time as the small group coordinator at National

> ## How long must I cry, O Eternal One, and get no answer from You? (Hab. 1:2)

Community Church. It was a perfect situation. I lived above the church offices on Capitol Hill at 2nd Street NE, right next door to the deteriorated, boarded-up crack house at the corner of 2nd and F streets that we had recently purchased to convert into our dreams of a first-class, fully operational coffeehouse where the church and the community could cross paths. It was an exciting time to be working in both worlds, and it was a unique season in life when I was able to lean into two very different interests and passions. The commute was great; the Senate office was a seven-minute door-to-door walk, while my commute to the church office involved descending thirteen steps. My steps to and from the Senate often turned into measured and needed prayer walks. On some days, my new husband, Ryan, and I would surprisingly encounter each other on our return commute and finish the journey together, recounting the joys, frustrations, and disasters of the day while scheming up plans of frivolity and mischief for the weekend ahead.

The commute home on November 12, 2004, began like any other typical Friday night. Leaving behind the stress of politics, I packed my briefcase and started the brief transition to a new weekend. The rain had begun earlier that morning and had evidently been a steady stream for most of the day. I buttoned up my trench coat and pulled my umbrella out of my bag as I exited the Russell Senate Office Building.

Outside, the cold November rain continued to fall steadily as I carefully navigated the broken and buckled brick sidewalks in my heels. As I neared the green eyesore that would soon become Ebenezers Coffeehouse, I looked forward to the groundbreaking that we would celebrate in one week. Joy and gratitude flooded my soul, but evidently a different kind of flood had compromised the ground on which I was walking. I've never really known exactly how to describe what happened next. When you are walking on a sidewalk in the city, you never stop to consider the precision of your steps or stability of the ground underneath you; you just take one step after another. On this particular day, however, one of my steps seemed to go farther than usual. With one step, I was swallowed by the sidewalk.

Let me be clear. There was no preexisting hole in the sidewalk that I blindly or clumsily fell into. The ground was literally crumbling under my feet as I descended into the eroding walls of a sinkhole. As a quick historical point of interest, Washington, DC, was built on a swamp, so this kind of phenomenon should really not be so shocking— but shocked I was. As I fell though the ground, bricks and dirt falling with me, my mind immediately raced back to a moment in my past that felt vaguely similar, and I concluded I was once again being pulled into a sewage or storm-water conveyance system and was in imminent danger of being swept under the street. Yes, I've had that experience, as well, but I will save that story for another book.

When the flow of mud and brick subsided and I seemed to land in a place of momentary stability, I concluded that I was trapped in a seven-foot sinkhole. It was absolutely the weirdest thing that had ever happened to me. My first emotion was a rush of embarrassment. I was at the corner of 2nd and F Streets during rush-hour traffic right across the street from the busy parking garage of the Thurgood Marshall Federal Judiciary Building. Surely, dozens of people saw this comedy and would be running over to help, and that was the last thing I wanted. I just wanted to get out of the hole as quickly as possible.

I'm short, but I'm scrappy. To hoist myself out, I jumped, grabbed onto the bricks above me, and attempted to pull myself out as one might pull oneself out of a swimming pool. *No problem*, I thought, *as I am sure I still hold the elementary girls pull-up record at Cottage Hill Baptist School.* Unfortunately, my strength was not an ally. The bricks I tried to make my pull-up bar simply fell right down on top of me, along with a massive quantity of dirt and mud. No big deal. I had also been doing a little bit of rock climbing, so I would simply employ those skills.

No good. As I sought to find a good foothold, my once-shiny power heels poked right through the dirt.

One of my favorite classes during my environmental engineering program was soil dynamics. I came to the astute conclusion that the structural integrity of this soil had been compromised by all the rain throughout the day, and if I were to continue an escape attempt on my own, I would be in very real danger of burying myself alive.

I wasn't worried. After all, I was at the corner of 2nd and F Streets during rush hour. I was certain *someone* would dash over at any moment to help.

No one came. I decided to call Ryan, who worked about a block away and should be leaving work at any moment. I pulled my phone out of my briefcase, which was still on my

> **I just wanted to get out of the hole as quickly as possible.**

shoulder, called . . . and got his voice mail. I left a quick message asking him to call me back when he got a chance, and put my phone back into my bag.

I noticed that my umbrella was still dangling from the sidewalk overhead, so I grabbed it and started waving it to draw attention. This was a busy Capitol Hill intersection, during the busiest time of day. Wouldn't *somebody* see my distress signal? No one came.

At that moment, I made a decision to yell for help. Even though I've never had to call out for help in a moment of panic, I imagine that the word wells up in the gut and flies from the lips naturally and organically. But when you have to strategize an intentional yell for help, it feels extremely awkward. I would start to yell, "Help!" get about as far as breathing out the *H* sound, and then just burst out laughing in the pit all by myself. I felt so stupid. As time continued to march on, I found more and more motivation for yelling, "Help!"—not catalyzed by panic but by frustration and anger. How was there *no one* coming to help in this tragedy?

> Sometimes, life drops us in places of extreme hopelessness that seem insurmountable and inescapable.

How did no one see this? How long would I have to yell for help? Why did no one hear? I yelled at the top of my lungs . . . over and over again. No one saw; no one heard; no one came.

Eventually, I emerged from that hole, but I will save the rest of the story for later. For now, let's just stay there, because it's a picture of the desperation we have all felt at times. I was desperate, and that entire incident has become a teaching moment for me. Sometimes, life drops us in places of extreme hopelessness that seem insurmountable and inescapable. Sometimes we make mistakes and bad choices that hurl us into the pits. Other times, we are simply walking along, minding our own business, looking forward to what's around the corner, and we find ourselves knocked off course, out of control, falling into the muck and mire. It's not the result of sin or silliness; it's the result of the unfortunate reality that there is simply something wrong with the world. Things are not all right in the land of the living, and we are swallowed up in dejection and distress. I've also learned that in those moments, I try a lot of strategies for getting out. Eventually, I come to a place where I realize I can't get out on my own, and I need help. So I stir up the humility and the guts to yell out for help. It begins as a whisper from one self-assured and self-confident and evolves to the cry of one completely aware of the vulnerability and helplessness of her situation. The cry escalates from discomfort to despair.

The cry is met with silence. No one seems to hear. No one responds. For how long?

HOW LONG? AND WHY?

We've all found ourselves in situations and seasons in which we wonder how long we will be stuck there. In "kid time," certain seasons seemed like an eternity and were often accompanied with incessant requests to know how long the holding pattern would last—the week before Christmas, the drive to Disney World, sitting in time-out—how much longer? As I grew a bit, my holding patterns seemed to be much more significant—waiting for the day I could get the driver's license, waiting for those college acceptance letters, waiting for the phone call from the cute boy in the second row of fifth-period English. Cries of "How long?" spring from my lips today as I sit for hours in the DC Department of Motor Vehicles and as I wait for my chronically non-punctual friends at the movie box office. Those are all the cries of impatience in response to first world problems. There have been other moments, however, when I've cried out, "How long?" in response to the gross injustice I see in this fallen world and the apparent inattentiveness of a God I understand to be loving. When my dad went on strike during my elementary school years, I asked, "How long?" As I watched my dear friend Cathy battle cancer for years, I asked, "How long?" When I prayed for my friend Mike as

> **As Habakkuk embraced God's character, he was forced to wrestle with God's actions.**

he walked through the pain of church politics that would seek to destroy the reputation of a good man, I asked, "How long?" How long before the house is sold, the job comes through, or the healing comes? They are words of anguish in the midst of a world that is broken. Something has gone wrong, and good people are left hurt, confused, and clinging as much as possible to whatever hope they can find.

This is the place we find Habakkuk. The first verse of the book introduces us to its central figure and writer. He was most likely a temple priest, and his name may have been related to a fragrant plant in the Akkadian region of ancient Mesopotamia. Jerome and Luther explained that his name meant "to embrace" or "to wrestle."[1] From his writing, we discover that he lived in the very tension of those ideas. As Habakkuk embraced God's character, he was forced to wrestle with God's actions; and as he wrestled with God's actions, he embraced His character. He also wrestled with his own people, his doubts, and his uncertainties, but he recognized that to truly wrestle, one must also genuinely embrace. Habakkuk was desperately concerned about the state of his nation. He was living in the midst of a spiritual sewer and was concerned about the spiritual complacency and lack of holiness, so he cried out to God on behalf of his people, asking Him to intervene in his situation and bring revival.

Jerome, one of the early "church fathers," was a theologian and historian in the fourth and fifth centuries AD and is best known for his translation of the Bible into Latin. He is also the patron saint of librarians. Martin Luther was an Augustinian monk who spoke out concerning the abuses he saw in the Catholic Church in the 1500s, namely, the sale of indulgences. The posting and widespread distribution of his Ninety-Five Theses sparked the Protestant Reformation. Luther embraced Habakkuk's central theology that "the just shall live by his faith" (Hab. 2:4 NKJV). Luther also judged Jerome for his asceticism.

The first words out of Habakkuk's mouth come screaming off the page in familiar desperation: "How long?" (1:2). Clearly, he was a man who drove straight to the point. He didn't feel the need to approach God in some pietistic posture or with a preamble of meaningless words to try to flatter God. His heart simply cried out, "How long?" Enough is enough.

The Scriptures don't shy away from that question. In fact, it's asked more than sixty-five times in the biblical text.

God was even known to ask it on occasion. For instance, in Exodus 16:28, God pondered how long His people would refuse to follow Him. Similarly, in Numbers 14:11, He questioned how long His people would ignore Him and treat Him wrongly even after all of the miracles He had worked on

> # Habakkuk recognized that to truly wrestle, one must also genuinely embrace.

their behalf. Even Jesus appeared to display a bit of divine impatience when He complained to His dimwitted disciples, "How long must I be with you? How long must I put up with you?" (Matt. 17:17 NLT).

The psalmist turned the question around and dared to ask God, "How long?" at least ten times. Consider these examples:

> How long, O Eternal One? How long will You forget
> me? Forever?
> How long will You look the other way?
> How long must I agonize,
> grieving Your absence in my heart every day?
> How long will You let my enemies win? (Ps. 13:1–2)

> O Eternal God, Commander of *heaven's* armies,
> how long will You remain angry at the prayers of
> Your sons and daughters? (Ps. 80:4)

How long *will we wait here alone?*
Return, O Eternal One, *with mercy.*
Rescue Your servants with compassion. (Ps.
90:13)

When Isaiah looked around at the corruption and brokenness of his people, he asked God, "How long will this go
on?" (Isa. 6:11 NLT).

When we fast-forward all the way to the end of the story,
we hear the martyrs cry out in a loud voice: "How much
longer, O Lord, the holy One, the true One, until You pro-
nounce judgment on the inhabitants of the earth? Until You
avenge our blood?" (Rev. 6:10).

Habakkuk echoed the familiar question: "How long
must I cry, O Eternal One, and get no answer from You?"
(1:2). Then he moved from asking, "How long?" to a new
question: "Why?" He followed up with three specific questions (paraphrased):

- Why do You not save?

- Why are we faced with injustice in the world?

- Why do You put up with wrong?

These are not new questions. In fact they are the oldest
questions in the world and the fundamental questions of
humanity. Does God exist? And if so, why is there evil in
the world? Where does evil come from, and why do bad
things happen? One of these questions goes all the way back
to the book of Job.

Most scholars believe that Job was the first book of
the Bible actually written, and it focuses on the oldest

theological question in the world: Why do bad things happen to good people? Job lost all of his possessions and his family, and ultimately he lost the support and encouragement of his best friends. In the book, he asks why more than a dozen times. Why was I born? Why have You made me your target? Why do You hide your face and consider me Your enemy? Why should I not be impatient? Job had

> **Does God exist? And if so, why is there evil in the world?**

good reason to ask why. Both God and Satan agreed he was the most righteous man alive. Why should the good guys face such torment?

There is a striking parallel found between the two books, Habakkuk and Job:

> Though I cry, "Violence!" I get no response;
>> though I call for help, there is no justice. (Job
>> 19:7 NIV)

> How long, LORD, must I call for help,
>> but you do not listen?
> Or cry out to you, "Violence!"
>> but you do not save? (Hab. 1:2 NIV)

When we turn to the last chapter of Job, the questions end and God speaks. But the questions remain. In this book that focuses on the question of why bad things happen to good people, the author never provides an answer. Instead, we are given an opportunity to see a picture of Job's character, posture, and response.

The "why" questions are as prevalent in Scripture as they are in our own lives. The psalmist asked why as often as he asked, "How long?"

> Why are the people making plans to pursue their
>> own vacant and empty greatness? (Ps. 2:1)
>
> Why, O Eternal One, are You so far away?
>> Why can't You be found during troubling times?
>> (Ps. 10:1)
>
>> Why have You forgotten me?
> Why must I live my life so depressed, crying
>> endlessly
>> while my enemies have the upper hand?
>> (Ps. 42:9)
>
> Why am I so overwrought,
>> Why am I so disturbed?
> Why can't I just hope in God? (Ps. 42:5, 11)
>
> Wake up, Lord! Why do You slumber?
>> Get up! Do not reject us any longer! (Ps. 44:23)

The question was even found on Jesus' lips as He pulled Psalm 22:1 from His memory and screamed from the cross, "My God, my God, why have you forsaken me?" (Matt. 27:46; Mark 15:34 NIV).

Habakkuk used six different terms to describe the dismay and hopelessness of the situation: *atrocities, wickedness, disaster, violence, conflict,* and *controversy* (1:3). He also declared that the law is "powerless" (1:4), from the same Hebrew word used in Genesis 45:26 and Psalm 77:2 to describe a heart or hands growing dumb, respectively. Jeremiah, who also prophesied around the time of Habakkuk, made similar claims with similar language about the wickedness of the people.

Habakkuk joined the chorus of prayers that seek to know "how long" and "why." The rules weren't working and the bad guys were winning. He was desperate for God to show up and do what only God can do.

∘ ⊙ ◉ DRIVEN BY DESPERATION

Desperation can be a powerful motivator to run to God.

In the ninth chapter of Matthew we read stories of two very different people. They were different in background and in social standing. The first was the leader of the synagogue; such men were educated, religious, and respected at the center of society. The other was a woman who had suffered from constant bleeding for twelve years. Such women were considered sick and unclean, and were forced to the outer fringes of society. Life dropped both of them to a state of pure desperation. The synagogue leader's daughter had died; the woman was exhausted from more than a decade of unanswered prayers and vain attempts at healing. In desperation, both of them clung to the hope found in the whisper of a simple proposition . . . "if."

The synagogue official approached Jesus. "My daughter has just died," he boldly asserted, "but you can bring her back to life again *if* you just come and lay your hand on her" (Matt. 9:18 NLT, emphasis added).

The woman didn't say a word; she just reached out in desperate hope, for she thought, "*If* I can just touch his robe, I will be healed" (Matt. 9:21 NLT, emphasis added).

Both official and outcast clung to a glimmer of hope that a cosmic cause-and-effect chain reaction can be ignited by the mention of a simple "if." Man and woman realized that when faith steps into the equation, a whispered "if" can blow open the doors of heaven and bring us into a place of endless possibilities.

We can all appreciate the pain the synagogue leader faced and the hopelessness he felt. While not all of us have

> ## Desperation can be a powerful motivator to run to God.

walked through the tragedy of losing a child, we can understand why he was so desperate to connect with Jesus. The woman's story might not seem as gloomy. In fact, we may think her situation was inconvenient and uncomfortable but not life-threatening. Surprisingly, the book of Leviticus can help us:

> If a woman discharges blood for several days beyond her menstrual period or outside of it, then she will treat those days as if she were having her menstrual period and will be impure. Treat every bed she lies down upon during her irregular discharge like the bed she lies down upon while she is in her menstrual period. Anything she sits down upon will be considered impure just as it is

when she is menstruating. By the same token, any person who touches the items *she touches* will be impure and must wash his clothes and bathe in water and remain impure until dusk. (15:25–27)

Nothing could have been more humiliating for her than this disease. For as long as a woman was bleeding for any reason, she was considered unclean. This particular woman had been bleeding continuously for twelve years and therefore had been living in solitary confinement and social exile all that time. She was, quite literally, untouchable. Everything she picked up would be considered unclean. Anyone who came into contact with her or anything she had handled would be unclean for the rest of the day. No one wanted to be near her. No one wanted to be with her. She was completely isolated. Excluded. Avoided. She was still in the land of the living but not alive.

A dozen years. Unclean. Why?

Her situation had obvious relational ramifications. Specifically, how must it have affected her marriage? Some commentators have speculated that her husband would have divorced her. Others suggest that she would have been compelled to leave him. There were spiritual impacts. She couldn't go to the temple or the synagogue. The person who needed the presence of God most in her life couldn't get to it. To make matters worse, in that culture it would have been assumed that her condition was God's punishment for some sin she had committed. She couldn't come into contact with anyone or she would render that individual unclean. Everything she touched was infected with impurity.

How long? Twelve years.

There were financial impacts. This woman's story is told in all three Synoptic Gospels, and when Mark told his account of her story, he mentioned that she had been under the care of many doctors, but they had only made her worse. How much money had she invested over those years in search of medical cures . . . only to find her situation worsened?

The books of Matthew, Mark, and Luke are considered the "Synoptic Gospels" from from the Greek *syn*, meaning "together," and *optic*, meaning "seen." They contain many of the same stories, in the same order. John, on the other hand, includes different stories in different order, likely because his book was intended to make categorical theological statements about who Jesus was more than give a chronological account of His life.

The Talmud, a Jewish commentary on the Old Testament, lists eleven different possible cures for her ailment. One suggested remedy was to carry the ashes of an ostrich egg in a linen bag in the summer and in a cotton bag in the winter. Another recommended "cure" was carrying around a barleycorn that had been found in the dung of a white female donkey. If finding a white female donkey wasn't hard enough, imagine tracking its poop to find a barleycorn.

Desperation. It is experienced irrespective of title, position, or social standing. When ancient Bible scholars translated the Bible into Latin, they labeled this combination of stories as *desperation in extremis*.

⚬⚬● DRIVEN BY DETERMINATION

In the midst of desperation, the synagogue official and the hemorrhaging woman were also fueled by a relentless determination to bring Jesus into their situations. The official took his "why?" to Jesus, and the woman took her "how long?" to Jesus. They could have let their desperation be a hindrance, causing them to hide from Him in mourning, shame, or embarrassment. Desperation often drives us to look for answers in places that promise relief but offer only emptiness—alcohol, busyness, work, food, and so forth. However, the synagogue leader and the sick woman let their desperation propel them to Jesus because they were confident that He could change their circumstances.

Jesus can't seem to resist desperate determination. God has habits, and one of the habits we see in the life of Jesus is a consistent response to those who approach Him in desperation and confidence. Consider His reaction in each of these instances:

- Four men carry their paralyzed friend on a mat and lower him through the roof, in search of healing. Jesus sees their faith and heals the man because of their desperate determination.

- A tax collector climbs into a tree just to get a glimpse of Jesus, only to discover that Jesus is looking for him and will invite Himself over for lunch.

From blind Bartimaeus at the gate of Jericho to the woman who crashed a Pharisee's party to wash Jesus' feet to the story about a widow who drives the judge crazy until he acts on her behalf, Jesus cannot resist desperate determination.

Sometimes, the best thing to propel us toward Jesus is desperate determination: that potent combination of certain despair in your circumstances and humble confidence in Christ that draws His heart to you. Where does your desperation lead you? Does it lead you away from Christ or toward Him? When we come to the end of ourselves, we find Christ. And there, the possibilities are endless. What are we desperate for? Are we desperate for God's involvement, or simply for His advice? What if we were so desperate

> When we come to the end of ourselves, we find Christ. And there, the possibilities are endless.

for a move of God that we would be willing to go anywhere or do anything just to be a part of it? When God is in the equation, potential is beyond limits. Dirt becomes the medicine that heals, love becomes the best weapon we can wield, and the voice of God is heard in the cry of an infant.

One of the most poignant tales of desperation is a story that Jesus spun to help His followers understand the extravagant love of His Father. A young man begins in one place of desperation . . . the kind that sends ambitious and idealistic explorers running off to face the world with youthful zeal and reckless abandon. But then he winds up in a different place of desperation . . . the kind one experiences after running headlong into a string of bad decisions that dead-end at the pigpen. He decides to crawl back to his father and beg to be enlisted among his servants. We can feel his embarrassment, pain, and regret because we've all found ourselves

> **When God is in the equation, potential is beyond limits.**

in that place at least once or twice. The story is labeled in many of our Bibles as "The Prodigal Son," but that's a bit of a misnomer. While the son certainly gets the largest amount of time on the stage, it is the father on whom the spotlight shines. While the son walks home with head hanging and shoulders sagging, the father, who has been looking from the window with expectancy, breaks out into a full sprint to embrace his son—not as a servant but as the guest of honor. Desperation drove the boy home, and desperation sent the father running.

What questions are haunting you? To what place of desperation has life dropped you? Habakkuk let his questions and his desperation drive him to his knees in prayer.

◦ ◦ ◉ STILL IN THE PIT

I fell with a briefcase into a pit on a rainy day. Obviously, I emerged relatively unscathed, and it's tempting to go ahead and tell the tale of escape. But let's just stay there for a moment in order to listen to the dialogue between Habakkuk and God. We love a good ending, but often we must walk through time and trial before we arrive there. Sometimes, our questions of why and how long are met with silence. Other times, they are answered in ways we did not anticipate and cannot comprehend. Such is the story of Habakkuk.

QUESTIONS

1. As you read the first four verses of Habakkuk, what resonates with you? What strikes you as odd?

2. Have you ever been angry at God? If so, why?

3. Habakkuk asks two primary questions: "How long?" and "Why?"

   a. What "How long?" questions are you asking in your own personal life right now?

   b. What "How long?" questions are you currently asking about the general nature of the world and times in which we live?

   c. What "Why?" questions are you asking in your own personal life right now?

    d. What "Why?" questions are you currently asking about the general nature of the world and times in which we live?

4. Describe a time when life dropped you into a pit that seemed inescapable. What was the resolution? If you are still there, what is your prayer?

5. Are you in a season of embracing God or a season of wrestling with God? How do those two concepts work together?

6. When people ask you how a good God could permit evil in the world, how do you respond?

7. Read Matthew 9:18–27.

    a. Is it possible to be too pushy or demanding of Jesus? What's the difference between being determined and being demanding?

    b. What principles can you learn from the determination of the synagogue ruler and the unclean woman?

    c. In what situation in your life have you trusted everything but Jesus? What would it look like for you, practically, to trust Jesus instead?

8. Turn your "why?" and "how long?" questions into a prayer list to use through the course of this study.

NOTES

CHAPTER THREE

PRAYERS GONE WILD

Take a look at the nations and watch *what happens*!
  You will be shocked and amazed.
For in your days, I am doing a work,
  a work you will never believe even if someone
    tells you *plainly*!
Look! I am *provoking and* raising up the bitter and
    thieving *Babylonian warriors* from Chaldea . . .
    (Hab. 1:5–6)

•❂❂ THE END OF INNOCENCE

We heard the news at church. If God didn't "intervene" and
"work a miracle," Brian would lose his leg the next morning.

I didn't know Brian very well. He was one of the older
kids at school, so the rules of grade school and middle school

social stratification had never allowed for interpersonal engagement. But I certainly knew who he was, and I had a vague awareness that he was sick. Not the kind of sickness that involves the intake of nasty medicinal syrups in exchange for a day home from school. A very serious sickness, like the kind that adults would talk about in hushed and grave tones when they thought the kids were playing in

> ### Take a look at the nations and watch
> ### *what happens!* (Hab. 1:5)

another part of the house. It was called cancer. When the pastor shared this "prayer need" in the middle of the service, faith welled up in my young heart, and some external wisdom seemed to convince me that God would absolutely "intervene." Why wouldn't He? I resolved in that moment to pray all night for God to show up. It was my first experience of believing God for something and recognizing the role I could play in the story that He was writing. I was convinced Brian was going to be healed, and my prayers would play a role in his healing.

It was a summer night, so my parents allowed my younger sister, Laura, and me to "camp out" in my room. That meant we got to sleep on the floor in our sleeping bags, and it was okay if we stayed up giggling a little longer than normal. This particular night needed to be different, though. I was focused and serious. Once my sister drifted off to sleep, I needed to pray. And pray hard. We were part of a denomination that did not speak of or witness miracles often. Certainly we saw a certain brand of miracle—angry people found joy, failing marriages found hope in Jesus, people who had no money discovered they could trust in God's provision. When a baby was born, that was a miracle. When a person was "reborn" in Jesus and baptized, that was also a miracle. However, the other kinds of miracles I read about in the Bible—the really cool ones, like people getting healed and food multiplying and storms subsiding—we just didn't really see those. We prayed for them, but it often seemed we prayed to have the grace to walk through the inevitable rather than having the faith to witness the reverse of the impossible. Occasionally, a missionary would come home from the field and tell us an amazing tale that seemed to fit more into the reality of New Testament life than the normal, everyday experience of our modern church lives, but those were typically received with a courteous smile and nod that recognized that all missionaries were a little goofy or a condescending acknowledgment that God sometimes had to show off His power to get the attention of the heathen. Not with us. He already had our attention, so we didn't need all that power stuff.

I was a third grader and didn't know any better, though. My theology had not yet "matured" to a place where I didn't need all that power stuff. My theology was pretty simple. First, I believed that what the Bible said about God was true. Over and over again, I was told that the Bible was the book that told us what to believe about God, and in that book, God healed people all the time.

Second, I was told that the God of the Bible had not changed, so the God to whom we prayed was the same God to whom David and Moses and Peter prayed. That also meant there was no reason to believe that fish couldn't be multiplied and dead people couldn't spring up out of graves today.

Finally, I believed that God answered prayer. The stories of the Bible were as real to me as the conversations that had happened on the playground the day before, and the characters of the Bible were as familiar to me as my friends. As far as I was concerned, David could have killed Goliath on my school playground yesterday. My little brain held absolutely no doubt that God would heal Brian if I prayed ardently enough and long enough. I would pray all night from that moment until the time of Brian's scheduled surgery. I snuggled into my Mickey Mouse sleeping bag, grabbed hold of my teddy bear, and settled in for a long night of prayer. I wasn't really sure how I would find enough words to pray all night, but I was committed.

It started with a little shameless pleading: "God, please heal Brian. Please, please, please heal Brian." It involved some explanation: "I know You heal people. I know You can do things that doctors can't do. The doctors can't do anything else, so Brian is going to lose his leg tomorrow if You don't heal him." I even tried a little arm-twisting: "I know You are going to heal him. And then everyone will know You are God!! That will be so great! All the people at the hospital will love Jesus because of what You did!" Finally, I threw in some words to let Him know I was serious: "I really, really want to see You heal Brian, and I'm going to prove it by staying up all night." Then I just started to repeat myself, but I said the words with more intensity and urgency. I could feel my faith rising with every word. This was going to be the most epic night I had ever experienced. God was not just giving me a front-row seat to a miracle; He had invited me to play a critical role. I prayed as I had never prayed before, and I prayed longer than ever before. I prayed for what seemed like an eternity. Granted, I probably only lasted a good fifteen minutes before my best intentions fell victim to the overpowering lure of sleep, but I was thrilled to be a part of something that God was doing that was going to amaze everyone. It was the first time I had come to a place of knowing something about God's character and absolutely believing that He could and would do something powerful and miraculous.

> I prayed as I had never prayed before, and I prayed longer than ever before.

The next morning, Brian lost his leg.

It was a defining moment. This was not one of those mysterious moments when God didn't answer a prayer. It wasn't a time when God seemed particularly distant, uninvolved, or uninterested in what we were asking for and so our prayers just seem to float in the airspace between earth and heaven. This was a definitive yes-or-no moment, and the answer was a resounding "No." Loud and clear. God could heal Brian, but He didn't. For some reason, God did not want to heal Brian the same way He healed all those people in the Bible. It was a defining moment for me and another instance in a mounting list of experiences that marked the end of innocence. Santa Claus wasn't real, the checkbook didn't provide free money, and God answered prayers badly. I was growing up, and it was all part of the maturing process. In this case, it was an opportunity for the kind of maturity that causes us to mentally excise the miraculous portions of the Bible. We may not literally take out our scissors and remove the miraculous sections, as Thomas Jefferson did, but emotionally and mentally we still remove them from our belief system.

The *Jefferson Bible*, also titled *The Life and Morals of Jesus of Nazareth*, was assembled by Thomas Jefferson by cutting and pasting sections of the Gospels together. Notably, he removed miracles, all mentions of supernatural occurrences, references to Jesus' divinity, and the resurrection.

I tabled that process for a season, though. Brian's amputation didn't make me mad at God or bring me to a crisis of faith. I didn't feel an urgent need to figure it out; I was just confused. I still loved God and knew He could do powerful stuff, but something had clearly gone wrong this time.

As the years passed, I learned that theology was supposed to be more complex than my simple three-part framework. I also learned there were basically two camps I could fall into to explain my badly answered prayer. I could have landed in either the camp that embraced the notion that God no longer really did that kind of stuff and my prayer was misguided, or the camp that embraced the belief that God was more than

> I still loved God and knew He could do powerful stuff, but something had clearly gone wrong.

happy to heal but my prayer just needed to be backed by more faith. Either postulate could have been true. On one hand, I never really saw God do any miracles like that, although I had heard the stories from those goofy missionaries. On the other hand, maybe my prayer was simply not good enough. After all, I had committed to praying all night, and I simply didn't do that. I decided I needed to find contentment in the somewhat noncommittal and in-between theological no-man's land that dismissed these difficult moments on the basis of "the will of God." We could understand Brian's tragedy within the framework that God could heal but chose not to for some inexplicable reason that it was simply not His will. None of those answers made any sense to me. Ever.

PRAYERS GONE WILD

When Habakkuk complained that God had made him look continually at injustice, God told him to broaden his gaze and look farther, beyond his own circumstances: "Take a look at the nations and watch *what happens*! You will be shocked and amazed. For in your days, I am doing a work, a work you will never believe even if someone tells you *plainly*" (Hab. 1:5). That was the answer the prophet Habakkuk received when he prayed a prayer of desperate determination: "Why do the bad guys win, and how long can You continue to let evil exist?"

> ## God told Habakkuk to broaden his gaze and look farther, beyond his own circumstances.

Why? And *How long?* Those are questions that all of us would love for God to answer. And if God had answered me the same way He answered Habakkuk—"Watch what I'm going to do, and be amazed"—I would have been thrilled. So excited, first, that God had shown up and spoken to me personally. And second, that He was giving me inside information and an invitation to experience the great work He was planning to do in the world. In fact, this is how this passage of Scripture is preached sometimes, and it goes something like this: "God is going to do something really awesome, so be on the lookout for it. It's going to blow your mind, and you won't be able to believe it!"

As we continue to read, however, we discover that God's instructions to "look," "watch," and be "shocked" and "amazed" are words of warning, not words of rescue. God's plan is not entirely what Habakkuk expected. Context is important. It's one thing to read that God is going to do something amazing, because that fits neatly into our theology and understanding of who God is and what He does. It's another thing to keep reading and realize that this alleged amazing thing doesn't seem good to us or for us. It's like the time Ryan told me our date night was a "surprise," and the surprise turned out to be a Marc Anthony concert. It wasn't the kind of date night you keep as a surprise because Heather is going to be beside herself with glee; it's the kind of date night you keep as a surprise because Heather may decide you can go on a date with someone else to that particular event (I love bluegrass, rock, and opera. Salsa . . . not so much). Habakkuk was facing a surprise slightly worse than Marc Anthony. God declared that the way He was going to bring change and set the wrong things right was by sending the Babylonians into Judah to conquer them. Amazed? Yes. But in a way that left Habakkuk completely confused.

What do we do when God's actions don't match how we perceive His character and promises? How do we respond when He doesn't behave according to our preferences? How do we process the moments when God's actions collide with our expectations?

Do we have a faith that is able to stand the test of life?

The Brian experience was my first Habakkuk moment. It was a badly answered prayer that didn't seem consistent with what I had read in the Bible or what I had been taught about God's character. The *why* question began to plague me, and for years I became numb to the phenomena of badly answered prayers. In fact, there were times it seemed as though, like Habakkuk, the harder I prayed, the worse things got.

● ◎ ● THE TERRIBLE, AWFUL, NO-GOOD BABYLONIANS

Habakkuk started in a bad place, characterized by violence, wickedness, disaster, conflict, and controversy. The bad guys were winning, and God seemed to be unaware of or disengaged from the situation. Initially, the prophet was concerned about his own people and wanted God to bring revival. After God answered, however, the situation went from bad to worse. The answer to Habakkuk's prayer for God to bring change was an invasion by the worst enemy imaginable—the Babylonians. They were exponentially worse than the Israelites, but God was going to let them win, and He didn't hide the horror that was coming. In fact, He was pretty explicit about their character and ways.

> **Eternal One:** Look! I am *provoking and* raising
> up the bitter and thieving *Babylonian*
> *warriors* from Chaldea;
> they are moving out across the earth
> And seizing others' homes *and property in their path.*
>
> That nation is terrifying *people,* is feared *by everyone.*
> It makes the rules and serves only its own
> interests. (Hab. 1:6–7)

Just in case Habakkuk wasn't already aware of how terrible these people were, God made it very clear. They were ruthless, impetuous, feared and dreaded thieves who were full of themselves.

In God's vision to Habakkuk, He also went into vivid detail about their strategy:

Babylonia's horses run faster than leopards,
> are fiercer than wolves when the sun goes down.

Its horsemen rush ahead *with deadly force,* galloping
> great distances;
>> the troops swoop down like eagles ready to
>> devour,

And Babylonia *keeps on* coming, *hungry* for violence.
> Hordes of *determined* faces are on the move *like a*
> *hot* east *wind,*

Scooping up captives like sand.

Their leader mocks kings and ridicules those in
> authority.
>> He laughs at every fortress

And builds ramps of dirt *against their walls* to
> capture it.
>> He blows through like the wind and then presses
>> on *to the next attack.*
>> For their king, his god is his strength, but he
>> will be held responsible. (vv. 8–11)

The imagery is graphic. The horses and troops were compared to leopards, wolves, eagles, and desert winds; thus, their armies marched at incredible speed. They were violent, they mocked authority, and they captured countless prisoners. The language of "scooping up captives like sand" makes one wonder if the prophecy contained a specific reference to the promise of Abraham that his descendants would be as numerous as the grains of sand (Gen. 22:17). Even the most well-built and stable cities were no match for the Babylonians' military engineering skills. They had defeated the Assyrians in 612 BC. In 605 BC, they had crushed the Egyptians and Pharaoh Neco at Carchemish. Nebuchadnezzar, king of the Babylonians, then pursued the enemy forces more than 150 miles to deliver the final crushing blow. When he heard that his father, Nabopolassar, had died, he raced hundreds of miles home to secure his throne.

> God described the Babylonians as ruthless, and we see an example of that in 2 Kings 25. When Nebuchadnezzar invaded Jerusalem, he captured King Zedekiah and his sons. He killed all of the king's sons in front of him and then gouged his eyes out.

They jeered and taunted enemies and relied on and worshiped their own strength. The Babylonian king Nebuchadnezzar certainly epitomized one who worshiped himself. In Daniel 4:30, he declared, "Isn't Babylon a great city? I have built this royal residence *from the ground up* with my own might and ingenuity to honor my own majesty." Later, he would build a statue to represent his glory and demand that his leaders fall down to worship him.

Nebuchadnezzar's palace was extravagant:

The palace complex was lavishly furnished and enclosed with a wall 136 feet thick. In the outer course of the wall, Nebuchadnezzar had his name inscribed on each brick. The terraced hanging gardens are said to have been located in the north-east angle of the palace complex and were considered to be one of the seven wonders of the ancient world. It is understandable, then, that Nebuchadnezzar named his palace "The Marvel of Mankind."[1]

These are the self-absorbed people God would send to bring correction to His people. Amazing. Even more, confusing. People who were far more wicked than the people of Judah were God's chosen instrument to bring correction to Judah. The prophet had hoped for a message of salvation, but instead he received a message of more judgment. His cries about violence are answered with more violence. It was not a new concept. From the time of Noah, there was an understanding that human life was precious: "Whoever sheds the blood of a human, that person's blood will be shed in return by another for God made humanity in

> ## The prophet had hoped for a message of salvation, but instead he received a message of more judgment.

His own image" (Gen. 9:6). Perhaps the "eye for an eye and tooth for a tooth" rule from the Levitical code sprang to mind. Instead of grace, Habakkuk discovered the horror of a punishment that fit the crime as the psalmist described in Psalm 7:16, "The trouble they cause recoils on them; their violence comes down on their own heads" (NIV). And yet in these situations, it was unfathomable that an even more wicked person would be the one to inflict judgment on the unrighteous.

● ● ● GRACE GONE MISSING

When Habakkuk asked why God was tolerating evil, the answer he received only prompted more questions. There is a sugarcoated sentiment humanity likes to embrace and Hollywood perpetuates that insists that the bad guys lose and the good guys win. Always. But in real life, the bad guys sometimes win. In this situation, it was God's choice that the bad

> It's as though grace went missing when Habakkuk's prayers went wild.

guys would win, which didn't seem fair. It's as though grace went missing when Habakkuk's prayers went wild.

Jesus once told a story about the master of a large estate who needed to hire workers for his vineyard. He went to the market, made an offer to some men looking for work, and hired them to work the entire day for the normal day's wage. The agreed-upon wage was most likely one denarius. Later in the day, he needed more workers, so he went back to the market to hire some more men, telling them he would pay them whatever was "right" at the end of the day. This scene repeated itself two more times. At the end of the day, he lined them up in order of how long they worked. Those who worked for an hour were given the honor of receiving their pay first, while those who had worked an entire day found themselves at the back of the line. Undoubtedly, those men who had worked the entire day were exhausted and eager to be paid so they could return to their homes and families, but they had to wait. Perhaps their spirits began to rise, however, when those who worked for only an hour were granted a denarius—a day's wage—what they had been offered originally. If their math was correct and one denarius was granted for one hour of work, then they would be bagging twelve denarii for their full day of work. But as they approached the table, the foreman dropped into their hands one denarius. We can certainly guess their thoughts. *Wait just a moment! One denarius? For working twelve hours, in the hottest part of the day?! That's just not fair!* (Matthew 20:1–13).

We often find ourselves in similar positions, demanding that God give us what we believe He owes us. "I've been loyal to my boss and done everything with integrity, so why didn't I get the promotion?" "I've tithed, so why can't You make my finances work out a little bit better?" "I've kept myself pure, so why haven't You brought me a husband?"

God never claims to be fair any more than He claims to be nice. He claims to be good, faithful, just, and loving. What we so easily overlook in this story is the extravagant grace and generosity of the owner. No one was paid less than they originally expected, but some were paid much, much more. Maybe we shouldn't be so quick to question the unfairness of God. Maybe the unfairness works out in our favor in the long run. It is grace gone wild. He is a Father who loves extravagantly. He gives grace that overwhelms those who don't deserve it. Sometimes we just have to wait for it.

• • ● HOT COALS, TEENAGE PREGNANCY,
AND OTHER BLESSINGS OF GOD'S PRESENCE

Many of us long to hear the audible voice of God or would at least settle for that inaudible but unmistakable voice of God. We think life would be great if we could just know exactly what God was thinking and what plans He had in store for us. That makes me wonder how many of us have actually read the Bible. Or maybe it's just that we don't really believe the Bible is true. When I look at the Scriptures, it seems that hearing God speak is often synonymous with bad news and uncomfortable outcomes.

Isaiah's mouth was singed by a hot coal, Jeremiah was given a message to declare that would cause him to be seen as a traitor by his own people, John saw the four horsemen of the apocalypse, and Mary was told that being highly favored of God meant having a child outside of marriage. Moses trembled when he encountered God on Sinai, Joshua fell on his face before the Lord, and Daniel was overcome with exhaustion and illness after seeing the visions God gave him. Reading the stories on this side of history, we see clearly the sovereignty and awesome grace of God at work. However, when you are a teenage girl living in Nazareth, "God's favor" and being pregnant out of wedlock would seem to be two mutually exclusive concepts.

I'm guessing you've probably experienced this phenomenon at some point. Sometimes our prayers are met with silence, and those are difficult seasons to walk through. We wonder if God even hears us or sees us. We question the way we pray and our ability to hear. We wonder if our prayers hit the ceiling and fall back down. We just want God to say something . . . anything. Sometimes, God answers our prayers in ways that make us wish He had just stayed quiet. All of a sudden, silence is the sweetest sound we can imagine, because the answer we hear takes the situation from bad to worse. We wonder if the wires between heaven and earth have been crossed or if God is really who He says He is. Instead of questioning if God exists, we begin to wonder if He is good. You've prayed for God to show up, and those prayers have been answered with not just silence but bad answers. The cancer spreads. Your teenager is pregnant. Your husband files for divorce. You were praying for a raise

> ## We just want God to say something . . . anything.

but received a pink slip. Where is God? You wonder if things might have turned out better or at least maintained the status quo if you had never prayed for God's intervention at all.

What's our response? Do we pray more? Or less? Where does our desperate determination lead us? Habakkuk had approached God with prayer—a good prayer—the kind that would have been considered self-sacrificing, devout, and faithful. And he was met with very bad news. God would indeed bring change, but through the most unholy means Habakkuk could imagine. His prayers had gone wild, and God's grace seemed to have gone missing.

Habakkuk's response gives us guidance on how we can enter the ring and wrestle with God.

QUESTIONS

1. How does God's response to Habakkuk line up with what you would have expected?

2. Describe some prayers that you prayed that went wild:

   a. Prayers that were not answered

   b. Prayers that were answered badly

3. There are several possible theological explanations for why Brian wasn't healed. Which seems to be the right perspective to you? Offer your reasoning from Scripture and experience:

   a. God no longer promises healing.

   b. God would have healed if enough people had expressed enough faith in prayer.

   c. God can heal and sometimes does heal, but it wasn't His will in this particular situation.

4. The question was posited in the book, "Do you have a faith that stands the test of life?" How would you describe that kind of faith?

5. Habakkuk was told that the bad guys were going to win and it was God's plan that they do. Can you think of other places in Scripture when the bad guys won? Are there situations in which it was God's will that bad guys would triumph over good guys? Does that still happen

today? How do you understand that in light of passages such as Romans 8:28?

6. Read Psalm 37. What warnings and hope does it offer?

7. Read Matthew 20:1–13.

   a. Is God fair? Why or why not?

   b. Is there a difference between grace and fairness? If so, how do they differ?

8. As we look at Scripture, it seems that people who encountered the presence of God were somehow changed in the midst of it. Can you think of a time in which you were changed in God's presence?

9. Make a list of the situations in your life where you need God's presence now.

NOTES

CHAPTER FOUR

GOING THE DISTANCE

Have You not existed from ancient times, O Eternal
    One, my holy God?
Surely You do not *plan* for us to die.
You, O Eternal One, have made Babylonia Your tool
    for judgment.
    You, O Rock, have established that king as *Your
        instrument of* correction.
Your eyes are too pure to even look at evil.
    You cannot turn *Your face* toward injustice.
So why do You *stand by and* watch those who act
    treacherously?
    Why do You say *and do* nothing
When the wicked swallows up one who is more in the
    right than he is? (Hab. 1:12–13)

When I think of Aaron Welty, I think of a man who fights to keep freedom alive with superhero-like confidence and strength in the halls of power in Washington, DC. I'm grateful for the man who leads small groups through both the mythical and theological writings of C. S. Lewis and J. R. R. Tolkien. I'm personally challenged by the policy adviser who mentors the newly arrived young and idealistic

> *Surely* You do not *plan* for us to die (Hab. 1:12).

political aides and interns who descend upon Capitol Hill at the turn of each political cycle. As he rides to work each day in a futuristic, electric-powered FENX vehicle that he designed and constructed with his father, he looks more like a pilot in the Rebel Alliance of the *Star Wars* universe than a young theologian and politico. The résumé he has built over the course of his first three decades of life is impressive.

As is true of any superhero, there is quirkiness lurking underneath his business suit. He seems to speak of the worlds of *Star Wars*, Marvel Comics, and Narnia with the same level of familiarity he expresses as he speaks of his hometown. He rattles off the names of superheroes and the protagonists of Middle Earth with the same affection he shows when he speaks of his closest friends. He feels connected to those who have defied the odds and saved nations and generations, and he does so with good reason. He has defied the odds too.

Aaron was born in June 1982—ten weeks before his expected arrival—and his parents were informed he would not survive. If he did survive, he would surely be a burden. He would never walk on his own (he was diagnosed with cerebral palsy), he would be severely mentally deficient (due to the buildup of fluid and blood on the brain and the resulting cranial pressure), he would never be self-sufficient, and he would never accomplish anything in life. Or so they were told. Aaron's parents chose to ignore the devastating news and believed their son had potential that no one else saw.

Such began the life of Aaron Welty. His first memory includes his grandma, a teddy bear, and an oxygen tent. He spent most of his early years in hospital rooms where he was required to stay for three to six months at a time. Scars on his body mark medical procedures long lost to remembrance because he was so young when they happened. While other children stretched for T-ball practice, Aaron's muscles were being stretched by plaster and fiberglass castings to combat the cerebral palsy.

In the eighth grade, Aaron underwent surgery to lengthen leg muscles and to manipulate kneecaps. The procedure went well, but his digestive system began to fail during the recovery process. That pain was unlike anything Aaron had encountered before. Tests were run and doctors were puzzled; eventually, they determined that he had an intestinal blockage that needed to be cleared.

For several weeks, Aaron drank only water while his stomach was pumped daily. As time passed and his skin turned yellow, he cried himself to sleep, acutely aware that he was dying. However, in the midst of the pain, God gave him an assurance that was undeniable and unmistakable: Aaron would not come to the end of his life in that hospital.

He survived. At thirty-one, he continues to thrive. He walked away from two near-fatal car accidents and recently spent three weeks recovering from a worse-than-average bout with kidney stones.

When you ask him about his response to all of the difficulty he has encountered, he doesn't talk much about anger, frustration, and confusion. Instead, he points to God's grace and sovereignty. And while he has definitely sought God for healing, he states courageously, "I realized that the greater miracle is not healing but endurance and perseverance."

Aaron has entered into the ring with God and has gone the distance, round after round. When he talks about his faith, his story begins to sound more and more like those comic-book heroes he loves. "What the doctors never understood is that God was then (and is now) the central part of the equation," he says, "and when God reaches down and ignites the path of destiny within someone (whom He took the time to form and knit together), all bets are off; this cannot be quantified.

"It's why the doctors looked at me a few years after I was born and marveled that I was still on planet Earth."

●●● THE PROBLEM OF EVIL

Why does a good God allow evil to exist in the world? That is a question that is beyond my theological training, experience, and wisdom. It's also beyond the scope of this book, but we've got to acknowledge it. For years, great men and women of faith have wrestled with "theodicy," or the way theologians try to explain the existence of evil in the world. J. I. Packer offers a concise statement of what we know about evil: "God permits evil (Acts 14:16); he punishes evil with evil (Psalm 81:11–12; Romans 1:26-32); he brings good out of evil (Genesis 50:20; Acts 2:23; 4:27–28; 13:27; 1 Corinthians 2:7–8); he uses evil to test and discipline those he loves (Matthew 4:1–11; Hebrews 12:4–14); and one day he will redeem his people from the power and presence of evil altogether (Revelation 21:27; 22:14–15).[1]

Those are the truths and promises we know, but what we don't know turns into a seemingly insurmountable list

> I realized that the greater miracle is not healing but endurance and perseverance.
> —Aaron Welty

of questions that will be left for eternity to explain. Why does God sometimes intervene but leave us to our pain other times? Why do the righteous sometimes win because of their integrity and humility, but often the bad guys win because they lie, cheat, and get ahead? Why does evil so often seem to defeat good? I think it's okay to ask those questions. Moreover, I think it's necessarily human to ask those questions.

The problem of evil creates an environment in which we are faced with a choice. When we see evil winning, we can choose to run away from God or we can choose to run toward Him. While the prophet Nahum, a contemporary of Habakkuk, asked, "How can God love and judge?" Habakkuk asked, "How can God love and *not* judge? Moreover, how can He love and judge *in this way*?"

> ## We can choose to run away from God or we can choose to run toward Him.

In Habakkuk 1:12, the prophet dared to engage God once again, going toe-to-toe. First, he reminded God that He was the Eternal One, the Holy One, and the Rock. Each of these characteristics would make us expect a different response from God. Second, Habakkuk asked two more *why* questions. Earlier, he had asked, "Why do You force me to see these atrocities? Why do You make me watch *such* wickedness?" (v. 3). In verse 13, he asked, "Why do You *stand by and* watch those who act treacherously? Why do You say *and do* nothing when the wicked swallows up one who is more in the right than he is?" In other words, *why do You tolerate evil? And why do the bad guys win?*

At some point early in our childhood, we were sold a load of bunk about how cheaters never prosper and liars always get caught. In elementary school, we were told stories of George Washington cutting down a cherry tree and confessing his sin, and we nodded our heads in perceptive understanding that we could never be president if we lied. In high school, we were warned not to smoke, drink, have sex, or even hang out with people who did because some terrible and embarrassing tragedy would certainly befall us. There were many Friday nights I sat at home, eating popcorn and drinking a cherry cola, while all those other kids were out doing whatever it was I wasn't supposed to do, and they always seemed to have lots of fun and never got caught. When we enter the workforce, we decorate our offices with pithy statements about the importance of integrity, honesty, and transparency, only to discover that sometimes cheaters do get the promotions. While we establish rigorous frameworks for behavior modification, the bad guys are out there winning.

Standing amazed and confused doesn't happen only when cancer strikes or people pull out guns in schools. In fact, I've often found that I can handle the bigger issues of life and death better than I can handle the incongruities, frustrations, and inequities of everyday, walking-around life. It's not always about tragedy; sometimes we get most tripped up when bad guys trump us in the presentation of accolades or even the race to the prime parking spot. We often try to convince ourselves that faith is being happy and content with whatever God has spoken, but I'm not sure that is entirely true. Maybe that's even an indication of a lack of faith in some way. Perhaps faith is really about pursuing God in the midst of uncertainty.

THE CANAANITE CONTENDER

One day, a Syro-Phoenician woman approached Jesus to beg Him to heal her daughter.

"Lord, Son of David, have mercy on me! My daughter is possessed by a demon. *Have mercy, Lord!*" (Matt. 15:22).

Jesus ignored her. But she persisted.

Finally, His disciples had heard enough and urged Jesus to send her away. In an uncharacteristically rude manner, He simply retorted, "I was sent here only to gather up the lost sheep of Israel" (v. 24). He didn't even acknowledge her or answer her directly.

> ## Perhaps faith is really about pursuing God in the midst of uncertainty.

She then knelt before Him and pleaded "Lord, help me!" (v. 25).

That's a prayer gone wild, but Jesus' response was completely confusing: "It is not right to waste the children's bread by feeding dogs" (v. 26).

What was the problem? At this point in the story, Jesus had healed people throughout the region of Galilee. He had erased leprosy; healed Peter's mother-in-law; opened blind eyes; unstopped deaf ears; fed five thousand hungry followers; and walked on water. This woman's request wasn't too big; He'd already cast out a demon *and* raised a girl from the dead. And while He sounded ethnocentric here, He had already healed a Roman centurion's daughter. He wasn't ignoring her to honor a cultural divide of men and women; He had healed a woman's incessant bleeding. Did the Canaanite woman from Syro-Phoenicia know about all of these healings? Or was she acting solely out of determined desperation? We don't know from the text.

We can observe a few things about her character and approach. She declared Jesus' character, she postured herself in a position to receive, and she wasn't afraid to talk back. "Even dogs eat the crumbs that fall by the table as their master is eating" (v. 27). In other words, she acquiesced, *Fine. I will accept that I am a dog, so treat me like You would treat a dog, because the scraps from Your table will satisfy me.* She stayed in the ring, absorbed the punches, and harnessed the energy to redirect it for her own benefit. She was the original aikido master.

> Aikido is a Japanese martial art that is based on the idea of redirecting an opponent's force rather than attacking it head-on.

Jesus was impressed: "Woman, you have great faith. And your request is done" (v. 28). That's the end of the story as far as the biblical text is concerned, but I want to hear the rest of this woman's story.

When our prayers go wild, it's not about shrinking back into a state of despair. It's a time to lean in, talk back, and listen intently. We've got to stay in the ring and remember we are not the first people to wrestle with God.

● ● ● RULES OF ENGAGEMENT

Habakkuk stayed in the ring. He reminded God of His character, and he asked some pretty pointed questions: "Why do You tolerate evil? Why do You stay silent when evil wins?" It was the third and fourth times he'd dared to ask, "Why?"

The heroes of the Bible were those who had the stamina to go the distance. Jacob found himself in an all-night wrestling match with God. Job stood toe-to-toe with God even when stripped bare of everything he could call his own. Mary and Martha wrangled with Jesus over why He had neglected to show up to heal their brother. The Psalms are full of questions, complaints, and grievances. It seems that answers were rarely given, but God always revealed something about His character in the midst of silence. For Jacob, He was the redeemer and keeper of the promise. To Job,

> The heroes of the Bible were those who had the stamina to go the distance.

He revealed His sovereignty and transcendence. To Mary and Martha, He declared Himself to be the resurrection and the life . . . and proved it. In the Psalms, He was the rock, fortress, and deliverer who is worthy to be praised in and through all of life's circumstances.

Sometimes, I feel bad complaining to God. Can you be upset with Him when you know intellectually that He knows what He is doing? Do you ask for what you really want when you believe His ways are higher than your ways, so maybe He knows better? Sometimes I don't know what's off-limits in prayer. Can I tell God I'm angry with Him when I know I shouldn't be? Can you throw out a four-letter word in prayer? I wrestle with a lot of those questions, but Scripture gives us the play-by-play of several people who wrestled with God. In *The NIV Application Commentary*, James Bruckner asserts, "Questions and lament are part of a believer's burden, and honest dialogue with God is a necessary form of relationship with him . . . Lamentation and questioning are God's gift to the believer. They provide a pathway of honest faith and faithful conversation with him in horrible times."[2]

Here are some specific guidelines we can learn from Habakkuk's conversation. Consider them rules of engagement for wrestling with God:

STAY IN THE CONVERSATION

Whatever you do, keep the lines of communication open. Even if you don't hear anything from God, keep talking to Him and keep listening to Him. You may encounter moments when it feels easier to walk away, but you really don't have anywhere else to go. That happened to the disciples on a few occasions. In John 6, Jesus was at the height of His ministry. He had fed a crowd of thousands with a little boy's lunch, walked on water, and He was giving a compelling sermon on being the Bread of Life when things turned weird. Instead of wrapping up His message and leaving the bread talk as a helpful metaphor, He made it personal: "Unless you eat the flesh of the Son of Man and drink His blood, you will not know life" (John 6:53). Then He said it again to make it clear: "If you eat My flesh and drink My blood, then you will have eternal life and I will raise you up at the end of time" (v. 54). On this side of the cross, we understand He was alluding to the Passover and to Communion, but He didn't offer that clarification to His audience. Instead, He kept prattling on about the necessity to eat Him. That's just weird. Jesus' life would have looked much different if He had employed a good PR director in His band of disciples. The crowds walked away. Confused.

Jesus then turned to His disciples and asked if they were leaving too. True to form, Peter spoke up: "To whom shall we go? You have the words of eternal life" (John 6:68 NIV). Right or wrong, for better or worse, Peter reaffirmed his commitment to Jesus. There are moments when we really don't want to hang in there with Jesus, but we know in our guts that there is really no other way to go. We've been too impacted and we've got too much invested, so we are stuck.

Stay in the game. Stay engaged in the conversation.

DECLARE HIS CHARACTER

I wanted to title this section "Remind God of His Character." I am fully aware of the fact that He doesn't need reminding because He knows who He is, and even if He could forget, He would be able to recall it in His omniscience. But sometimes *we* forget, and His actions don't remind us. That's when we anchor ourselves in Scripture and declare His character in the midst of our circumstances. We don't let what we know about our circumstances tell us what is true about God; rather, we allow what we know about God to tell us the truth about our circumstances. We can either frame God with our problems or frame our problems with God. Do we view God against the characteristics of our predicaments or view our predicaments against the character of God? Don't just talk to God about the questions, challenges, and uncertainties you are facing; declare His character in the midst of them. Remind Him—but more important, remind yourself—of His character.

KNOW THE DIFFERENCE BETWEEN DOUBT AND UNBELIEF

In the opening scene of the play *Doubt*, Father Flynn declares, "Doubt can be a bond as powerful and sustaining as certainty."[3] Doubt can help us bond with God in a powerful way, so we must understand the difference between doubt and unbelief. While doubt compels us to run to God to debate, complain, argue, and question, unbelief causes us to abandon God. When Jesus challenged the rich young ruler to sell everything he had and give to the poor, the young

> We can either frame God with our problems or frame our problems with God.

man didn't push back with questions to clarify Jesus' meaning. He just walked away. He couldn't believe. Compare that story to the one about the father of the demon-possessed boy. When Jesus pushed him to demonstrate more faith, he declared in desperation, "I do believe; help me overcome my unbelief!" (Mark 9:24 NIV). This is an example of the kind of faith-filled doubt that many of us need to embrace. It's a faith that keeps a desperate grip on hope despite the fact that it defies our logic and emotions. God doesn't appear to grow upset or impatient when we challenge Him, question His actions, or second-guess His perfect will. Even Jesus seemed to second-guess the Father on the night of His crucifixion when He asked if there was any way possible for the cup of suffering to pass Him by. That was just a much more eloquent way of second-guessing God's plan. But it wasn't unbelief; He submitted and committed to the Father's will

> ## Doubt can be a powerful catalyst to faith.

despite the outcome. In His prayer to abandon the plan, there was not a shred of His being that would consider abandoning the Father's will.

Doubt can be a powerful catalyst to faith. If you are wrestling with God, doubt can be a good thing because it demonstrates you have not walked away from Him. Warren Wiersbe states, "To avoid tough questions, or to settle for half-truths and superficial pat answers is to remain immature, but to face questions honestly and talk them through with the Lord is to grow in grace and in the knowledge of Christ."[4]

In *The NIV Application Commentary*, Bruckner offers the following distinction: "The faithful protest begins with an attitude that continues to address God ('God, how could you allow . . . ?'). The unfaithful protest begins with the impersonal (and judging) abstraction ('How could God allow . . . ?')"[5] Doubt and unbelief are characterized by two postures: Doubt questions God. Unbelief accuses God. Habakkuk asked lots of questions about God's actions, but he never accused God for His actions. Doubt engages; unbelief walks away.

ACKNOWLEDGE HIS WISDOM AND LOVE

The final rule of engagement I try to employ is to recognize that I am not as smart as God is and I am not as loving as He is. I can identify so many moments when I question God's wisdom or wonder about His love because His actions don't seem very smart or loving to me. That's when I have to remember that I'm just not as loving as God is and I'm certainly not as smart as He is. That seems ridiculously obvious to state, but usually that's the issue when I have a complaint against God. The Scriptures declare that He is love—not just that He loves or does loving things but that He is the essence and perfect embodiment of love. By definition, anything and everything He does is loving. God is also smarter than me and has a perspective that I don't have. Romans 8:28 declares, "And we know that in all things God works for the good of those who love him, who have been called according to his purpose" (NIV). Some have interpreted this verse to mean "God is going to make it all better," but it really means "God is carrying out His purposes exactly as they are meant to be fulfilled; nothing is by accident." We want God to work according to our expectations, but He works according to His purposes. What seems best to us may not be what is best for us because He has a perspective that we don't have.

● ● ● RESURRECTION

Revelation 3:20 reminds us that God is willing to go the distance and be persistent with us first, before we ever decide to serve Him: "Now pay attention," He says. "I am standing at the door and knocking. If any of you hear My voice and open the door, then I will come in to *visit with* you and to share a meal at your table, and you will be with Me."

I always imagined that verse as a onetime salvation moment. Jesus knocks, and we either open or close, and that's the end of the story. Maybe that's too simple. Perhaps it's better understood as a promise. Sometimes He knocks and we just yell at Him to go away. Then He knocks again

> We want God to work according to our expectations, but He works according to His purposes.

at some point and we reply with a slightly more refined but just as assertive "No, thank you." Perhaps another time He knocks and we crack the door, poke our heads out, and respond with a slightly irritated "What do You want?"

Yet, God remains persistent.

Aaron Welty stands as a monument to God's persistent grace. As Aaron has opened the door of his life to his Creator and Sustainer, God has opened doors for him in very influential environments.

The doctors had pronounced him as good as dead, but Aaron's parents chose to listen to different voices. The odds were stacked against him, and life has knocked him down a few times, but Aaron consistently picks himself back up, squares his shoulders, locks eyes with God, and dares to embrace Him once more.

Today, Aaron has endured thirty years of wrestling with God, but he clings to 2 Corinthians 4:7–10 to make sense of it all; he recognizes he is simply a clay pot in which Jesus' *"resurrection* life *rises and* reveals its wondrous power."

In John 11, we see a vivid description of a God who breathes life back into the dead. The metaphor that may help us understand Him best is that of a surgeon. He knocks you out and then cuts into you with a knife. You are laid out on a table, helpless, bleeding. Strip away the familiar hospital environment and the white scrubs that betray the occupation and the surgeon might be mistaken for a madman, a sadist of incomprehensible evil, whose heart beats without a single drop of human empathy. However, when understood against the backdrop of the hospital, the mad sadist transforms into a skilled and meticulous caregiver. The surgeon is understood only as someone who is good, who knows what he is doing, whose scalpel moves with precision and intentionality to bring life to what was dead.

● ◉ ● FISH TALES

The first chapter of Habakkuk ends with a fishing metaphor to describe the ruthless cruelty of the Babylonian army:

> But the Babylonian yanks up his enemies with a
> hook,
> dragging them away with his net.
> Gathering them up like fish in a net,
> the king shrieks and shouts for joy at his catch.
> So he offers a sacrifice to his net *that has made him
> rich*;
> the smoke of his sacrifices rises for his fishing
> net *that has brought him success*;
> Because of it, his table is full and his belly is fat.
> Will he empty *and fill* his net *without end*?
> Will he continue to murder the people of the
> world without pity? (1:15–17)

The fisherman's net was a sign of military strength, and it was an object that the Babylonians worshiped. It was a symbol of what brought them success. Meanwhile, the fish were the helpless masses upon whom they preyed. It is here that Habakkuk shifts gears and prepares to listen to God once again, posturing himself for the blows that may come.

QUESTIONS

1. What names and attributes did Habakkuk declare in his response to God?

2. Read Matthew 15:21–28. How is this woman's story similar to Habakkuk's? How is it different?

3. Consider the following rules of engagement: staying in the conversation, declaring God's character, knowing the difference between doubt and unbelief, and acknowledging His wisdom and love.

   a. Which one is the easiest for you to do?

   b. Which one is the hardest for you to do?

   c. What would you add to this list?

4. When Jesus told His followers they would have to eat His body and drink His blood, many of them couldn't bear it and deserted Him. The Gospels are full of hard sayings of Jesus. What are some things that Jesus taught or instructed that you wish He had not said?

5. What aspects of God's character do you need to embrace most during this season of your life? What are some practical ways you can maintain a growing awareness of them?

6. How would you describe the difference between doubt and unbelief? What doubts are you struggling with right now? In what areas are you struggling with unbelief?

7. What is the difference between questioning God and accusing God?

8. Do you believe God is smarter than you and more loving than you? If so, why?

9. Make a list of situations in which you need to pray to God, "Help me in my unbelief."

NOTES

CHAPTER FIVE

WRITE IT DOWN

I will take my place at the watchtower.
I will stand at my post *and watch*.
I will watch and see what He says to me.
I need to think about how I should respond to Him
When He gets back to me with His answer.

Eternal One *(to Habakkuk)*: Write down this vision.
Write it clearly on tablets, so that anyone who
reads it may run.
For the vision points ahead to a time I have
appointed;
it testifies regarding the end, and it will not lie.
Even if there is a delay, wait for it.
It is coming and will come without delay.
(Hab. 2:1–3)

Sometimes we question God's goodness when tragedy strikes and the foundation of life crumbles beneath our feet as we crash into the abyss of suffering. Other times, we find ourselves questioning God as we fly through the air . . . only we suddenly start flying faster than we had wanted because life popped the fabric of our hot-air balloon. We thought we were having fun and soaring high above the earth only to discover that someone poked a hole in our fun.

God doesn't seem fair when the good die young or when tragedy strikes innocent people. He also strikes us as unfair in the more mundane moments of life when the kid who

> *I need to think about* how I should
> respond to Him (Hab. 2:1).

didn't study for the test sets the curve and the kid who didn't practice gets fourth spot in the batting order. Several years ago, my friend Brad interviewed for a position with an organization that sought to influence Capitol Hill through kingdom principles. The person hired for the role would build relationships with Capitol Hill staffers, launch Bible studies to build community for staffers, offer classes on Christian worldview and the role of faith in politics, and create environments where people who were not followers of Jesus could meet Him. Because Brad was already leading Bible studies with Hill staffers, had worked in the political arena for several years, and knew the details and daily challenges of Capitol Hill life, he was well qualified for the job. As we prayed together, we were both convinced that he would have right of first refusal, but someone else edged him out, a kid who had just graduated college and had no experience in DC or politics. Brad was told the other guy was just "slightly more qualified." We could only laugh and assume his "qualifications" were based solely on someone he knew in an influential position. Brad would wait several more years before he finally landed in a role where he could do the kind of ministry on Capitol Hill he had hoped to do.

Obviously this is not a tragedy. The pain over a lost job opportunity certainly doesn't rise to the same level of confusion and pain as some of the other stories we know, but it's one of those moments that generates frustration and leaves us confused about God's actions (or inactions). Against the backdrop of eternity, it is no big deal; but in the momentary reality, it just doesn't make sense and it's not fair. What's the right response?

Habakkuk finished his complaints and questions and went to the watchtower to await God's response. His prayers had gone wild; he was plagued with doubts, questions, and uncertainties; and God's actions had collided headlong with his expectations. What do we do when we've expended all of our energy, registered all of our complaints, and asked every question we can think of, and God's actions still don't match His character and promises as we perceive them?

God was willing to go another round with Habakkuk because He is always willing to go another round with those of genuine hearts and sincere questions. Habakkuk postured himself for a response by listening and watching. While most prophets understood their role to watch how the people of God would respond to and keep God's covenant, Habakkuk postured himself to see how God would respond to and keep His own covenant. He needed to think about how he should respond to God, so he climbed up the ramparts on the city walls to look for God and listen to Him. His experience sounds very similar to the one recorded in Isaiah 21:1–12. After walking around naked and barefoot for three years to deliver a message to the Egyptians and Ethiopians about the imminent invasion of Assyria, Isaiah received a new message about the "Sea of Wilderness *(Babylon)*" (v. 1).

> ## Habakkuk strategically positioned himself in the best possible place to seek God.

The vision was so frightening that Isaiah used graphic language to describe his own terror: "My stomach sinks. My gut churns with pain . . . *I can hardly bear the news* . . . I'm bent over with agony . . . I'm deep in the fog of depression" (v. 3). Isaiah's response was to stand guard at the watchtower day after day. Ezekiel and Hosea also positioned themselves in watchtowers to hear from God (Ezek. 3:17; Hos. 9:8). Likewise, Habakkuk strategically positioned himself in the best possible place to seek God.

God spoke again: "Write this down." Don't miss it. Don't get distracted. Don't forget it. "Vision" comes from the Hebrew word *chazon*, which literally means "something seen."[1] Sometimes the prophets would write their visions on large wooden tablets so everyone would be able to read their messages (a couple of examples can be found in Isaiah 8:1–4 and Isaiah 30:7–8). These tablets functioned like an ancient message board in the town square or a public service announcement on the radio or the bulletin board at the local coffeehouse. God told Jeremiah to write His words in a book (Jer. 30:2). In Habakkuk, God wanted the vision written "clearly" so that those who read it could "run" (2:2). There's been a bit of debate among scholars over the exact interpretation of those words. Does God want one who is running to be able to read it clearly and quickly? Does He want one who reads it to immediately run to carry and proclaim the message to another? Does He want the one who reads it to be able to run well in his or her journeys in the promise and hope He is offering? Either way, God wanted the message to be stated with clarity so those who read it would walk in the understanding and with the assurance that He would do exactly as He promised.

Before God explained further, He encouraged, *Wait for it. I'm going to make everything right, but you are going to have to wait for it. You've got to stay in the right posture, and you've got to be patient.* Waiting was not a surprising position for the prophets of God.

HERDING SHEEP

God seems to favor shepherds. Honestly, I've never been really excited about that idea. The image of shepherds in my head is the really nice guy carrying the peaceful demeanor on his face and the little white lamb around his shoulders. That just doesn't strike me as a role I could get very excited about. That's the job for the people with mercy gifts, who like to feel deeply with people, love animals, and favor introvert time. I always saw the shepherd as the kinder, gentler leader. I wanted to be more like Deborah . . . out on the battlefield and beating people up for the glory of God and His kingdom. That was before I spent a little time in the wilderness home of the Old Testament shepherd.

I've been to Israel twice, and both times, I was transformed in the paradoxical land of the wilderness. On one hand, it's deserted and lonely; but on the other hand, the

> ## Waiting was not a surprising position for the prophets of God.

presence of God seems so tangible that you believe you could actually reach out and touch it. The desert is also eerily quiet, yet you are convinced that if your ears were tuned to the right frequency, you could literally hear the rocks crying out their praise to God at a deafening decibel level. The wilderness is hard, rocky, and hot. The terrain is tricky to navigate, and the environment is difficult to endure. This is the turf of the shepherd, the landscape in which we would have found all of the recipients of the Old Testament covenant promises—Abraham, Moses, and David. It's where we would have found the other patriarchs, Isaac and Jacob, and the prophet Amos. After His baptism, Jesus voluntarily admitted Himself into a wilderness experience. All of them lived for at least a season of their lives in the vast emptiness of the wilderness. In that place, I discovered a new respect for this tribe who could nail lions and bears (and when appropriate, giants) with a slingshot with pinpoint accuracy. Shepherds were a hardy bunch who learned the lessons of the wilderness, or "God's classroom," as it has been called. It's a place where God sent people who would one day lead others; He sent them there to listen, to learn, to grow closer to Him, and to develop the character they would need to sustain their calling.

All of us find ourselves in wilderness seasons. Typically, we immediately run to the prayer, "God, get me out of the wilderness." Given what is revealed in Scripture, the better prayer might be "God, what do You want me to get out of the wilderness?" The goal is not figuring out *how* to get out of the wilderness but *what* to get out of the wilderness. Posture and patience are two of the lessons of the wilderness, and they were also the strategy of Habakkuk.

POSTURE

There were no lone rangers in the wilderness because you had to lean into one another and rely on one another because you never knew when and where the rains were going to come or where the pasture would be. The wilderness requires a spirit of humility.

Moses was called the most humble man who ever lived (Num. 12:3).

David was anointed king of Israel, defeated Goliath, and won the favor of the people, but refused to lay a hand on King Saul. David was willing to follow a man who was difficult to like and impossible to respect because he trusted God to get him where he was supposed to go.

If we ever wonder what the correct response might be in any situation, humility is always the right answer. If we concentrate on having the right posture before Jesus, God will ensure we attain the right position before men. Our job is to posture ourselves on our knees and let God take responsibility for determining what position we have before others.

In Philippians 2, we are given insight into the posture that Jesus took.

> Don't let selfishness and prideful agendas take over. Embrace true humility, and lift your heads to extend love to others. Get beyond yourselves and protecting your own interests; *be sincere,* and secure your neighbors' interests first. *In other words,* adopt the mind-set of Jesus the Anointed. *Live with His attitude in your hearts. Remember:*
>
> > Though He was in the form of God,
> > He chose not to cling to equality with God;
> > But He poured Himself out *to fill a vessel brand new;*
> > a servant in form
> > and a man indeed.
> > The very likeness of humanity,
> > He humbled Himself,
> > obedient to death—
> > a merciless death on the cross! (Phil. 2:3–8)

Humility isn't thinking less of yourself; it's thinking of yourself less. If we are genuinely seeking the highest good of another person, we are living in humility. To place someone else's needs or preference above our own is an expression of humility.

A second practical way to understand and demonstrate humility is to do the little things as if they are the big things.

I am not good at that. While God has tried to teach me this lesson over and over before in my life, I became most cognizant of it when I first moved to DC about fifteen years ago. A member of the United States Senate invited me to be a part of his staff to focus on his work on the Senate Environment and Public Works Committee. He had asked me because I had a graduate degree in environmental engineering, and he was particularly interested in some research I had done on the issue of climate change. An everyday Christmas-party conversation about global-warming potentials of methane, the significant injection of aerosols into the stratosphere from the climactic 1991 eruption of Mount Pinatubo, and

> ## Humility isn't thinking less of yourself; it's thinking of yourself less.

the complexities of atmospheric chemistry prompted him to ask me if I would be interested in working in the Senate for a year. When I arrived, there were a number of fascinating hearings on the schedule to prepare for. There were people to meet and speeches to write and legislative architecture to design.

My first job: to archive my legislative director's files from the previous Congress.

I didn't know it at the time, but the legislative director (LD), who serves as the chief legislative architect for the senator, admitted to me later that he gave me that job because

he didn't like me even before he met me. He had resented
the fact that the senator had hired someone for his team
before consulting him, and he wanted to put me in my place.

I was shocked. I was a little disappointed because I was
really excited to jump right into energy and environment
policy. I was a little ticked because I had passed on two perfectly good job offers that would have paid three times as
much money to come archive files. More nobly (or was it nar-
cissistically?), I was concerned that the senator's wishes were
not being fulfilled. He had brought me on board because of
my expertise, and it was a waste of my gifts and knowledge
to relegate me to the file cabinet. To make matters worse,
the files were a mess, and my LD would carelessly dump files
on the floor for me to deal with.

Nevertheless, I had recently taught on Daniel's character. He had done little things as though they were the big

> Do the little things as if they are
> the big things.

things, and that caused others to notice his character and
then to recognize his gifts. I begrudgingly decided to be like
Daniel . . . or maybe it was just that I wanted to prove how
good I was . . . so I filed. I did that stupid job with excellence
and efficiency. Later, my LD apologized for giving me that
assignment, but I think he was right. I absolutely needed
to learn my place. Not to mention that the filing ordeal
proved to be one of the most important jobs I did all year. It

gave me access and insight into the senator's entire history of legislative architecture, and I learned all of the senator's positions and language. By the end of the year, I had been trusted on issues outside my area of expertise because I had been given the opportunity to be a student of the structure and framework of the senator's policy strategies.

There is an interesting legendary connection between Daniel and Habakkuk. The apocryphal Bel and the Dragon, an addendum to the book of Daniel not included in the Old Testament canon, tells the story of Habakkuk taking food to Daniel in the lion's den.

I didn't enjoy one minute of that work, and I mumbled under my breath the entire time I was doing it. But while I was on my knees, getting paper cuts all over my hands and hauling box after box, in heels, to the archive attics of the U.S. Senate . . . God was positioning me for something down the road.

You would think I had learned my lesson, but fast-forward fifteen years, and I am still relearning it. Recently I stumbled onto a Monday morning task list left on the desk of one of my coworkers. This particular coworker is one of the oldest and most experienced members of our team. Before coming to National Community Church, this individual held a high-ranking position at Naval Criminal Investigative Service (NCIS). Previously, he had been a legislative fellow for a U.S. senator and led NCIS teams and initiatives around the world. With this résumé, this is not what you'd imagine his Monday morning task list might include:

- Stock copier and printer paper
- Stock paper towels in bathroom
- Clean up table next to printer

It continues to describe the weekly e-mails that need to be sent, the people with whom he needs to connect, lessons he needs to prepare, and so forth. But he begins his week by stocking paper, cleaning the printer table, and stocking the bathrooms. To my knowledge, no one asked him to do that. He just does it. He does the little things as if they are the big things but doesn't make a big deal about it.

Humility means we make a big deal about Jesus . . . not a big deal about ourselves. Then we are in the right position to hear and receive whatever God may say to us.

PATIENCE

Some scholars think the book of Habakkuk is a compilation of conversations between the prophet and God over a period of time. What takes us a few minutes to read may have been the summary of a few days, weeks, or even years of conversation between the two. Sometimes, conversations with God seem to take forever; we want answers immediately. Furthermore, while His voice sometimes speaks slowly, His actions, at times, seem to be glacial.

In Exodus 13, the children of Israel had been delivered from Egypt and were beginning their journey to the promised land. They hadn't quite reached the Red Sea when we read this: "After Pharaoh sent the people out, God did not take them by the *coastal* road that runs through the land of the Philistines, even though that was the nearest *and easiest* route. Instead, God said, 'For if they see battle *with those contentious Philistines,* they might regret their decision and then return to Egypt.' So God *chose a different, longer path that* led the community of His people through the desert toward the Red Sea" (vv. 17–18).

God intentionally took the Israelites on the most indirect path to ensure they went on the best path. The point: God isn't in a hurry. He isn't in a frenzy trying to figure

> You have all the time you need to accomplish all the work God wants to do in you and through you.

out how in the world He can do everything He wants to do in your life. You have all the time you need to accomplish all the work God wants to do in you and through you. You learn patience in the wilderness. Abraham waited decades for Isaac. Moses spent forty years in the desert . . . and then went back for more. Our most direct path of progress is not always God's desired path of growth. Where you are going and what you are doing is not nearly as important as who you are becoming.

Henry Cloud offers this perspective on the temptations of Jesus in the wilderness: "Think of what the devil did in the temptation (Luke 4). He offered Jesus instant relief from His hunger, but Jesus said no. He offered Jesus instant glory, but He refused. The devil offered Him instant safety, but Jesus rebuked him. Jesus knew that to gain those things, He had to go through a process that was God's way. And He learned obedience through the suffering."[2]

Again, when we find ourselves in the wilderness, the next step is not to strategize a way out of it, but to find out what we are supposed to take out of it. We tend to regret yesterday and worry about tomorrow. Or we yearn for yesterday and reach for tomorrow. All the while, we are distracted from seeing what God has planned for us today. I am convinced that one of the reasons God does not reveal His full plan to us when we want it is because we wouldn't be able to handle it. We would either shrink back in fear or insecurity or be puffed up in pride. Humility takes time . . . and time requires patience.

WRITE IT DOWN

We live in the world of microwaves, movies on demand, and one-click shopping. The promises made to me as a child by my favorite eating establishments included "having it my way right away" and "fast food for fast times."

Impatience can impede the work that God wants to do in us and through us. In 1 Samuel 13, we find that Saul is facing the Philistine army at Micmash. The prophet Samuel had instructed the king to wait for his arrival so he could offer sacrifices and ask for God's favor on the Israelites. The Philistine army was impressive—"30,000 chariots, 6,000 horsemen, and so many foot soldiers they were like grains of sand on the beach" (v. 5). Saul's army began to flee in terror. After seven days, Saul was tired of waiting, so he gathered the offerings and made the sacrifices himself. That was the beginning of the end of Saul's reign and the favor of God upon his life (vv. 13–14).

Abraham didn't wait for a son, and the choices he made led to history-changing sibling rivalry. The prodigal son didn't wait for his inheritance, and the choices he made led to the temporary loss of blessing. Judas couldn't wait for Jesus to establish the kingdom, and he traded his eternal inheritance for thirty pieces of silver.

> Impatience can impede the work that God wants to do in us and through us.

We've lost the art of posture and patience, and yet some of the verses we love to quote the most require patience. Perhaps God's answer reminded Habakkuk of David's cry in Psalm 37:7, "Be still. Be patient. Expect the Eternal to arrive *and set things right*. Don't get upset when you see the worldly ones rising up the ladder. Don't be bothered by those who are anchored in wicked ways."

He may also have recalled the words of the prophet Isaiah from a generation before: "Since ancient times no one has heard, no ear has perceived, no eye has seen any God besides you, who acts on behalf of those who wait for him" (Isa. 64:4 NIV).

In Exodus 14, God's battle plan for the newly delivered Hebrews was . . . to do nothing. Moses stood between the Red Sea and the Egyptian army and delivered his prebattle pep talk: "Do not be afraid. Stand firm and you will see the deliverance the LORD will bring you today. The Egyptians you see today you will never see again. The LORD will fight for

> **Patience is the best way to combat the enemies of our hearts and minds.**

you; you need only to be still" (vv. 13–14 NIV). Sometimes patience is the best way to combat the enemies of our hearts and minds.

David waited for God to elevate him to the throne, and God declared him a man after His own heart (1 Sam. 13:14; Acts 13:22). Isaiah encouraged that those who waited on the Lord would renew their strength (Isa. 40:31). The disciples waited for the Holy Spirit in Jerusalem, and by His power, they healed the sick, raised the dead, and spread the gospel all over the Roman Empire (see the book of Acts).

Waiting is a spiritual discipline. Henry Blackaby once said that what he needed most was "unhurried time with God."[3] There is a difference between acting out of a sense of urgency and acting out of a sense of hurry. Jesus moved with urgency, but not with hurriedness. He was about the Father's business . . . not busyness.

Waiting is also a gift, but it's a gift we fail to accept. It lets us recalibrate, breathe, and actually look. Waiting reminds us that the earth doesn't stay in orbit because of us. The molecular structure of all matter and the gravitational forces of the world will not crumble if we are not running at the speed of light. The speed of life is what God designed us to run, and it reminds us that God is in control and we are not.

When we take God's plans into our own hands, we discover trouble. Whenever we try to take shortcuts, we short-circuit the ultimate call He has placed on our lives. We may wonder *why* and we may ask, "How long?" and we may watch in confusion as the bad guys get ahead, but our response is to watch what God might say and wait for Him to answer. Write it down. Do not forget it. Do not get distracted. He is never early and He is never late; He is always right on *His* time. Wait for it.

QUESTIONS

1. What were Habakkuk's next steps? What was God's answer?

2. We must have faith in the significant trials in life, but we must also have faith during the trivial and mundane frustrations, inconveniences, and disappointments of everyday life. Where do you need to have faith regarding the trivial matters?

3. Instead of praying "Get me out of this situation" prayers, we should pray "What do you want me to get out of this situation?" prayers. What is a situation you have been trying to escape that God might want to use as a classroom

environment to teach you something? What are some practical things you can do to be more mindful of what God might want you to "get out of" the circumstances you are in?

4. Read Philippians 2. Make a list of the character traits Jesus displayed.

5. If humility is not thinking less of yourself but thinking of yourself less, what are some practical things you can do to develop humility in your life?

6. What little things do you need to start doing as if they are big things? Who will hold you accountable to that?

7. Read Daniel 1. What principles do you learn from the lives of Daniel and his friends?

8. Practice the discipline of waiting on God this week. Each day, spend ten minutes simply listening.

NOTES

CHAPTER SIX

LIVING FAITH

> *. . . but the righteous shall live by his faith.*
>
> —Habakkuk 2:4 (ESV)

•◦◉ PHONE CALLS OF FAITH

The telephone is an incredible invention. It is morally neutral yet history defining. Think about the decisions and news that have been conveyed over the telephone. In 1876, a new era of communications began as Alexander Graham Bell made the first phone call to Thomas A. Watson. On July 19, 1969, President Nixon made the longest-distance phone call to Buzz Aldrin and Neil Armstrong on the moon. My own life-changing move to DC was initiated by a phone call on Easter Sunday. What was meant to be a phone call to give a life update to my pastor turned into a ministry calling. Phone calls informed me that my niece had been born and my granddaddy had passed away. And it was a series of phone calls that taught me something about faith.

I don't remember the first time I met Marva Adams, but I do remember the first time I met her daughters. They were both at the young adults retreat I attended four weeks after first visiting National Community Church. The youngest, Christy, drew the short straw to be my cabinmate. I'm convinced it was the sovereignty of God because Christy and her sister Leslie both became dear friends, the kind that only come along a few times in life.

> **Faith is the assurance of things you have hoped for, the absolute conviction that there are realities you've never seen (Heb. 11:1).**

A few years later, their aunt Joan began to battle cancer. I don't remember ever personally meeting Joan, but I was impacted by her kindness. When I moved back to DC in 2001, I crashed in the spare room of the Adams house for a few weeks, and Joan bought some temporary furniture because I was "going to need a place to unpack" my things. When I heard she'd lost the battle, I slipped out of the conference I was speaking at in Gulf Shores, Alabama, climbed onto some rocks, prayed, and made one of the hardest phone calls I had made to date. The Adamses are good people, and it all seemed so illogical. Heartbreaking.

Months passed, and as Ryan and I realized that our dating relationship was heading in a potentially permanent direction, we mutually decided to find an older couple to mentor us. We didn't really know what we wanted in a mentoring couple; it just sounded like something good to have. Our families are very important to both of us, and it seemed foreign for us to navigate an important decision such as marriage without the encouragement and counsel of parents nearby, so we primarily wanted some surrogate parents close by to augment the parental wisdom we were getting from afar. Independently, we prayed for a few days about who we would like to approach to fill that role, and we came together with mutual agreement. We wanted Gregg and Marva Adams to mentor us.

On a separate note, I had been praying for a mentor for several years. I was still working full-time in the U.S. Senate and part-time for NCC, and I knew I was entering a season of transitions and big decisions. I just wanted an older woman to walk alongside me. Marva was a win-win for my life. We loved the Adamses, my parents loved them, and Ryan's parents loved them. For several months leading up to our engagement and marriage, they loved us, prayed for us, encouraged us, and were available for all of our ridiculous questions and concerns. Gregg told me once he had rarely known Marva to open up as much as she did for me. I don't know that I fully understood that or appreciated it at the time.

Then cancer struck again. This time, it was Marva. Lightning couldn't strike the same family twice, could it? Deep down, I knew Marva would come through. Her mom was still living, she had two daughters, and she loved life. She and her husband hopped on a plane and celebrated our wedding in Mobile.

A few months later it seemed as if things took an unexpected turn for the worse. In February, I went to the hospital to visit and was shocked to find Marva in a coma. The night before, she had gone to dinner with friends, full of energy and life. A few days later, Christy called me at work. "Heather, I was just called to the hospital. It doesn't sound good. Could you just pray?" She assured me I didn't need to come with her. About an hour later, my phone rang again. This time, it was Pastor Mark. "Marva has passed away, and

> **I was confused by what God was thinking and doing.**

the family asked me to call you." The speed at which she left us was incomprehensible.

The next few days were a flurry. I saw an amazing picture of the love and support that the body of Christ provides, but I was confused by what God was thinking and doing. To me, He was the bad guy of this story, but I didn't have time to think about that or even talk to Him about it. I had small groups to console, a family to prepare food for, and a eulogy to write. It was cathartic to be busy helping others mourn and cope. Meanwhile, my heart ached. I was angry, but I could channel that energy into serving others and playing the pastor. Eventually, life began to move on again, and I couldn't hide behind the pastor role anymore. I was left with questions and a hollowness of heart. How could God take away such a good person? Why would He make a mother bury not just one but two daughters? How could he take away a mother just years before her own daughters were married? And on an incredibly selfish note, what about me? For one thing, I didn't want to pray for another mentor; I just wanted Marva back in my life.

There was only one thing that made me pause every time I started to let God have it: the faith of the Adams family. Gregg, Leslie, and Christy displayed a calm in the middle of a storm like I had never observed before. Certainly, it was difficult. Surely, when no one was around, they questioned and cried out in frustration. They hurt just like anyone would in those circumstances. But they had faith beyond their circumstances. In fact, their lives were anchored by it and framed by it.

They lived by faith.

LIVING BY FAITH

In the second chapter of Habakkuk, God responds to the prophet's protest: *Write it down. What I say will happen is going to happen, and there are two ways to live through it. The enemy lives with pride and selfish desires. The righteous will live by faithfulness.* Another translation would render it "The just shall live by his faith" (NKJV).

The message takes an abrupt turn here as God moves from pronouncing the coming destruction of Judah to the later destruction of the Babylonians themselves. Verse 4 declares, "Look at the proud! They trust in themselves, and their lives are crooked" (NLT). The NIV translates it, "See, the enemy is puffed up; his desires are not upright." In the original Hebrew language, "puffed up" is a peculiar expression that carries with it the idea of being swollen—the prideful serve their own interests and worship their own strength as a god. It can also indicate a loss of faith.

According to Rabbi Simlai (a third-century teacher), "Habakkuk based all the 613 commandments received by Moses on the single principle that 'the righteous shall live by his faith' (Hab. 2:4; Mak. 23b–24a)."[1] This simple idea, tucked away in the middle of banter between God and an obscure prophet, found its way into three New Testament letters and became a catalyst for the Protestant Reformation. John Calvin said it is "that faith which strips us of all arrogance, and leads us naked and needy to God, that we may seek salvation from him alone, which would otherwise be far removed from us."[2]

> They had faith beyond their circumstances. In fact, their lives were anchored by it.

This declaration about the relationship between the just and their faith has been translated four different ways in Hebrew, LXX, and New Testament quotations:

- "living by faith"
- "living by faithfulness"
- "living by [God's] faith (or promise) concerning the future of the righteous"
- "living by [God's revelation's] faithfulness"

LXX refers to the Septuagint, a Greek translation of the Old Testament. It was likely translated sometime around the second century BC and is quoted by many New Testament writers, particularly Paul. It was also heavily used by the early church fathers and continues to be the version of the Old Testament used in Eastern Orthodox churches.

If you read commentaries, you will find a good bit of debate over the correct translation and the differences between faith, faithfulness, and the faithfulness of God. Is their disagreement over the understanding? Or is the original language so layered and kaleidoscopic that we find dimensions of our faith, our faithfulness, and God's faithfulness working together to form a more complete picture? Perhaps living "by faith" and living "by faithfulness" are not two mutually exclusive ideas. *The NIV Application Commentary* posits that perhaps the "perceived contrast" between the two ideas is in reality a "false dichotomy."[3] Faithful living and sturdy faith are indivisibly linked. I struggle with this idea every time I stand in line for a roller coaster. If I have faith that the roller coaster will not fly off its track and into orbit, then faithful living will lead me to strap myself in and enjoy the ride. If I have faith that a bridge will hold me but don't take a step to cross it, then I am not living by faith. (Sidewalks are another story . . . and I promise to get back to that.) If I have faith that God is who He says He is and will do what He says He will do, then that will change the way I live my daily life. James Bruckner explains it this way:

"Faith is what faith does. 'Living by faith' is redundant because faith is lived faith when someone is faithful . . . The one who trusts God in faith lives faithfully by his Word. Conversely, the one who is faithful to his Word also clearly trusts it and has faith in the One who gave it."[4]

The words "live by" that precede the word "faith" or "faithfulness" further bolster the notion that we are not simply embracing an idea or a mind-set. This isn't just about giving mental assent to an abstract principle; we are living as if we believe something is true. One principle of scriptural interpretation is to "let scripture interpret scripture." In other words, when the meaning of a passage is confusing or unclear, look for other places where a common word or

> ### Faithful living and sturdy faith are indivisibly linked.

theme is addressed to see if it sheds new light or gives more insight into understanding. In the case of Habakkuk 2:4, we find three notable places where it is quoted in the New Testament. Pastor and author Warren Wiersbe summed it up: "It takes three books to explain and apply this one verse."[5]

Galatians, Romans, and Hebrews are arguably the three most theological books of the New Testament. In the book of Galatians, Paul framed the way that law and grace interacted, and he took his first stab at a systematic theology, which would later be fleshed out in the book of Romans. Hebrews was written by someone, likely a Levite, to lay theological groundwork for devout Jewish people who were considering the claims of Christ. When Paul quoted Habakkuk in Galatians and Romans, he emphasized that by faith a person is justified. The writer of Hebrews, on the other hand, stressed that by faith a person who has been justified will live.

Let's unpack Habakkuk 2:4 in each of them.

HEBREWS

The author of the book of Hebrews wrote to a Jewish audience to make the case that Christ was the Messiah they had been waiting for. In many ways, it served as a sequel to the Old Testament book of Leviticus, demonstrating that Jesus is the perfect sacrifice, the great High Priest, and that His sacrifice marked the final and ultimate Day of Atonement. Specifically, he wrote strategically to encourage Jewish Christ-followers to remain steadfast in their devotion to Christ. Because Judaism enjoyed certain freedoms under Roman rule, the first Jewish Christ-followers were free to worship without fear of persecution. Once Christianity was viewed as constituting a *new* religion as opposed to a sect of Judaism, persecution flourished and many Jews considered abandoning their embrace of Jesus as Messiah and running back to a persecution-free form of Judaism. In chapter 10, the writer encourages them to be confident in their faith and believe God's promise.

> Remember this, and do not abandon your confidence, which will lead to rich rewards. Simply endure, for when

you have done as God requires of you, you will receive the promise. *As the prophet Habakkuk said,*

> In a little while, *only a little longer,*
> the One who is coming will come without delay.
> But My righteous one **must live by faith**,
> for if he gives up his commitment,
> My soul will have no pleasure in him.

> *My friends*, we are not those who give up hope and so are lost; but **we are of the company who live by faith and so are saved**. (vv. 35–39; bold emphasis added)

The writer of Hebrews was encouraging a life of faith in difficult times, despite the fact that it is precisely because of our faith that we face persecution, imprisonment, or even death. Habakkuk told the people of God to have faith in the vision that the Babylonians would eventually be destroyed. In Hebrews, the people of God are encouraged to look to Jesus Christ as the hope, power, and promise of God for their ultimate salvation. In both texts, we are encouraged to live based on who God says He is and what He has done and to trust that He will be true to His promises regarding the future. Be "of the company who live by faith and so are saved" (Heb. 10:39).

GALATIANS

Paul most likely wrote his letter to the church in Galatia right after the Council of Jerusalem in Acts 15. Sometimes even the most well-meaning people with sincere hearts and genuine faith disagree over how we live out what we believe. The early church was faced with the question of the gentile Christ-follower. Some argued that one must become culturally and religiously Jewish to be a follower of Christ, while others argued that the gospel was for both Jew and Gentile and the real issue was a relationship with Christ. Paul was an ardent proponent of salvation by faith alone, so he argued that Gentiles were not required to become Jewish in order to become followers of Christ. He didn't mince words, charging Peter with "hypocritical behavior" (Gal. 2:13) and wishing that his opponents would "castrate themselves" (Gal. 5:12 NRSV). That's not exactly a bumper sticker memory verse, but it demonstrates Paul's fierce devotion to the gospel.

A precursor to Romans, Galatians is a very theological book, examining the right way to think about things like

> Sometimes even the most well-meaning people with sincere hearts and genuine faith disagree.

faith and salvation. It serves as a bridge between Old Testament thinking and New Testament living, and it encourages us to live in the freedom and power of the Spirit of God. In Galatians 3, Paul argued that the new covenant is mediated by Jesus Christ and the Spirit of God, not the Law.

> *Listen,* whoever seeks *to be righteous* by following *certain* works of the law actually falls under the law's curse. I'm giving it to you straight from Scripture *because it is as true now as when it was written:* "Cursed is everyone who doesn't live by and do all that is written in the law." Now it is absolutely clear that no one is made right with God

through the law because *the prophet Habakkuk told us*, "**By faith the just will obtain life**." The law is not *the same thing as life* formed by faith. In fact, *you are warned against this when God says,* "The one who observes My laws will live by them." *I am trying to tell you that* the Anointed One, *the Liberating King,* has redeemed us from the curse of the law by becoming a curse for us. It was stated *in the Scriptures,* "Everyone who hangs on a tree is cursed *by God.*" *This is what God had in mind all along:* the blessing He gave to Abraham might extend to all nations through the Anointed One, Jesus; and we are the beneficiaries of this promise of the Spirit that comes *only* through faith. (vv. 10–14)

Jesus is the perfect fulfillment of the Law, and He raised the bar. Outward allegiance to the Law was not enough; rather, an inward and radical righteousness necessitates a relationship with Jesus Christ. What we believe and how we act are inextricably linked. If we are people of faith, we will live faithfully; and faithfulness is living by faith. As we live in Christ, we will receive life by faith.

ROMANS

Paul sent a letter to the church in Rome to remind them that it wasn't about what they could do for God; rather, it was about what God had already done for them. Containing the New Testament's most comprehensive explanation of God's plan for restoring relationship with humanity, Paul systematically outlined the major doctrines of faith, focusing on God's grace, mercy, and humanity's reconciled and restored life in Christ. Romans is the book that comes closest to being a "systematic theology" in the Scriptures. Unlike the majority of Paul's letters, Romans was written to a church he did not plant and to a group of people he did not know. This letter became a major influence on the lives of Augustine, Martin Luther, and John Calvin and was a catalyst for the Protestant Reformation. The quotation from the book of Habakkuk, included very early in the book, provided the fuel:

> For I am not *the least bit* embarrassed about the gospel. *I won't shy away from it,* because it is God's power to save every person who believes: first the Jew, and then the non-Jew. You see, in the good news, God's restorative justice is revealed. *And as we will see,* it begins with and ends in faith. As the Scripture declares, "**By faith the just will obtain life**." (Rom. 1:16–17; bold emphasis added)

In some translations, the word "righteous" is used. In the Old Testament, people were not considered to be "just" or "righteous" because they were flawless and faultless. Righteousness was not about perfection, but it was revealed in the way one responded to God and to neighbor. Paul was eager to share the gospel because God's restorative justice involved faith in Jesus Christ. He connected righteous living (seeking to live uprightly in the community of God) with the righteousness of God (who is Jesus Christ). Our righteousness before God is found in Jesus Christ. As Paul wrote to the church in Corinth: "He orchestrated this: the *Anointed* One, who had never experienced sin, became sin for us so that in Him we might embody the very righteousness of God" (2 Cor. 5:21).

In other words, it's not about what we do for God; it's about what God has already done for us—which, in turn, changes everything we do.

● ● ● WHEN CHRISTIANS LIE

"Just tell me everything is going to be okay." That's all she wanted me to say, and it seemed simple enough.

I was driving back from New York City with a young leader, and for a few hours we talked about the particular challenges she was facing in her ministry, leadership, and relationships. We hashed through the advantages and disadvantages of potential upcoming opportunities and decisions

> It's not about what we do for God; it's about what God has already done for us.

and recognized that things could get worse before they got better. At the end of the trip, we found ourselves sitting on the sofa in my living room, and I asked a question that I often ask young leaders when I want to be there for them but don't know what that should look like practically: "What do you need from me?"

She answered simply: "Just tell me everything is going to be okay."

I paused for a moment, and then laughed with a response that shocked us both:

"Sorry. I can't tell you that. Hebrews tells us that some Christ-followers were mocked and beaten and stoned and sawed in two and thrown to animals. So, yeah—who knows what could happen to you?"

I wasn't joking, and I continued: "What I can tell you is that God is good, sovereign, and faithful, and a life given completely to Him will not be regretted."

"Just tell me it's all going to be okay." Just a little comfort and assurance was all she wanted. Just one little throwaway line to fill her heart with warm fuzzies and set her mind at ease. We Christians love to say that kind of stuff to each other, and certainly, in the eternal sense, it is all going to be okay. We know the end: Jesus wins, reigns eternally, and has prepared a place for us. However, in the here and now as we live in the land of the "now and not yet," we are not assured of anything but God's grace, goodness, faithfulness, and sovereignty. Admittedly, empathy is not one of my strengths, but I empathized deeply with her in that moment. I dug deep down into the most empathetic place in my heart . . . and refused to tell her it was all going to be okay.

Many of us love Hebrews 11. Listen to this faith-stirring passage:

> *I could give accounts of* people alive with faith who conquered kingdoms, brought justice, obtained promises, and closed the mouths of hungry lions. *I could tell you how people of faith* doused raging fires, escaped the edge of the sword, made the weak strong, and—stoking great valor among the champions of God—sent opposing armies into panicked flight. I could speak of faith bringing women their loved ones back from death. (vv. 33–35)

Yeah. That's the kind of faith I want to have and the kind of life I want to live. As a kid, my Sunday school teacher told me that Hebrews 11 was the "Hall of Faith," and I decided I wanted my name listed there, as well.

Conveniently, though, most of us never care to read or talk about the last five verses of this great chapter on faith. In fact, we stop halfway through verse 35. Keep reading from verse 35 on . . .

> I could speak of faith bringing women their loved ones back from death and how the faithful accepted torture instead of earthly deliverance because they believed they would obtain a better *life in the* resurrection. Others suffered mockery and whippings; they were placed in chains and in prisons. The faithful were stoned, sawn in two, killed by the sword, clothed only in sheepskins and goatskins; they were penniless, afflicted, and tormented. The world was not worthy of these saints. They wandered across deserts, crossed mountains, and lived in the caves, cracks, and crevasses of the earth. These, though commended by God for their great faith, did not receive what was promised. That promise has awaited us, who receive the better thing that God has provided *in these last days*, so that with us, our forebears might finally see the promise completed. (vv. 35–40)

These heroes were tortured, but they refused to turn from God. They were mocked and whipped and chained and stoned and gutted and sawed in two. None of them received all that God had promised . . . He had something better in mind. What do we do when we don't receive all that God promised?

In the first thirty-four and a half verses of Hebrews 11, we see the stories of those who found God to be the Deliverer. Their stories ended happily ever after. They believed God could and God would—and God did.

But in the second half of verse 35, we begin to find those who stood strong in faith in the midst of pain and torture—in the midst of being amazed and confused. They embraced a God who can and who will deliver but sometimes does not. They remained faithful anyway.

Stories of great faith always begin with great adversity. Faith does not mean God meets our expectations. It means we cling to God's character, knowing that God will always

> **Stories of great faith always begin with great adversity.**

accomplish His purposes. God wants to forge in us a faith that is far greater than our circumstances. Faith means knowing God can, believing God will, but clinging to Him even if He doesn't. Faith is not an assurance that everything is going to be okay; it is the assurance that God is in control. That's the only way to live, knowing that some of the pains and confusion of life will remain mysteries even to our graves. Reinhold Niebuhr said, "A genuine faith resolves the mystery of life by the mystery of God."[6]

● ● ● NINETY MONTHS

Ryan and I want children. That's the only thing we know for sure in the whirlwind of questions we are confronted with on the subject. Whether or not we will have them, how that will come to be, and how much they will reflect our unique DNA remains to be seen. Before we got married, we both had an unshakable notion that I was going to get pregnant quickly—on birth control or not. We shared a premonition that our debate between two or three children would prove to be a moot point as we slowly learned that God had created us with the reproductive skills of rabbits. We laughed about that a lot until year four, when we realized God was going to honor our birth control, and we decided to come off the pill. For about a year, we didn't try; we just stopped *not* trying. A year later, we decided to start intentionally trying. Then we tried harder. Then we tried tests. Now, in year five of waiting, we are in the land of decision about the next step.

I know women who have walked through this longer than I have and experienced pain worse than I will ever be able to imagine, and I would never assume I understand their stories or presume to tell them how they should respond to God or anyone else. All I know is what I've learned about myself and about God, and I have asked every question that Habakkuk asked:

How long? I know His timing is perfect, but why is it always so long? I know He is never late, and every other time I've had to wait has made sense in hindsight. But I'm closing in on my forties. The fact that Sarah gave birth to Isaac when she was ninety does not encourage me; that's frightening.

Why? I'm finding that the heart-level questions that I've barely found the courage to whisper are revealing what I believe about God. The question that haunts me the most is not necessarily "Why do I not have kids?" but "Why would God not let me have kids?" We all take "why" questions into eternity with us; I just want to make sure I carry the *right ones* with me. Whatever that means.

Why do the bad guys win? The teenagers having sex in the backseat of the car. The college student who will go to the abortion clinic. I remind myself that those people are not bad guys but people just like me who wrestle with difficult consequences and choices. I fully embrace a theology that

> Faith means knowing God can, believing He will, but clinging to Him even if He doesn't.

acknowledges both a world thrown off-kilter by sin and a God who is loving, not fair. But I also know a God who sometimes intervenes. Why not now?

Even now, all of those questions still linger, despite the fact that God is very talkative every time I bring it up to Him. Unlike Habakkuk, I haven't heard a bad answer; rather, I've been encouraged to be a spiritual parent, to trust in His timing, to be aware of all the wonderful opportunities I have because of my DINK (double income–no kids) freedom, and to remember that the Bible is full of stories of barren women who eventually gave birth to heroes. I have no idea how this story will end. I do know that God is good, faithful, and sovereign, and when those truths are difficult to see, I go back to those moments in my story where those truths were clear. I think Hannah was able to praise God so eloquently after Samuel's birth because she had ardently trusted God in faith before Samuel was born, not just for what she believed He would do but for who He was. She

> At the end of the day, God is still sovereign, faithful, and good.

trusted His character before she believed for His action. I can continue to ask how long, why, and why does God bless those who don't play by the rules, but at the end of the day, God is still sovereign, faithful, and good. It's the struggle and tension of living in the land of the "now and not yet" and the exciting and potentially painful anticipation of "if not" faith.

As Augustine said, "The faithful do not expect to hear from God what they desire, but to desire what they hear."[7]

QUESTIONS

1. How are faith and faithful living interconnected? Do we live faithfully because we have faith? Or do we develop faith because we live faithfully?

2. How would you define "faith"?

3. Read Hebrews 10:35–39. What does this passage tell us about Jesus? What does it mean to be "of the company who live by faith"?

4. Read Galatians 3:10–14. What is the difference between the law and the life formed by faith? What is the difference between following rules and living by faith?

5. Read Romans 1:16–17. How does Paul describe the "good news"? What is the role of faith?

6. Has your faith changed over time as you have followed Jesus? If so, how?

7. What lies have we either told or believed about how God interacts with us? What would be a better response to people facing uncertainties, disappointments, and tragedies?

8. Make a list of people who have set an example of living by faith. Write a letter to one of them to tell that individual how his or her life has served as an example and encouragement to you.

NOTES

CHAPTER SEVEN

WOES

Woe to him who hoards what is not his!
> How long can he profit from extortion *and
> debt?* . . .
Woe to him who builds his house on such evil
> profits,
>> who puts his nest up high, *safe for the future,* safe
>> from disaster! . . .
Woe to him who builds a city on bloodshed
> and who establishes a town by injustice! . . .
Woe to you who gives his neighbors a drink,
> who keeps filling their cup with your anger *and
> malice*
To intoxicate them so you can *uncover their shame
and* look at their nakedness! . . .
Woe to him who says to *a block of* wood, "Wake up!"
> or to a silent stone, "Arise!"
Are *inanimate* objects your teachers?
> Look, it may be covered in gold and silver,

But there is no breath *of life* inside.
But the Eternal One is in His holy temple.
Let all the earth keep silent in His presence.
(Hab. 2:6–20)

As if the first chapter of Habakkuk weren't bad enough, the second chapter is worse.

God now turns His attention from the devastation that is coming to Judah to enumerate the reasons why the Babylonians will ultimately be destroyed themselves. While the bad guys will win for a season, they, too, will eventually fall because of their lust for power and pleasure and their trust in lesser gods. Babylon is mocked with a lament—these are not curses but a song of ironic mourning for the people of

> **But the Eternal One is in His holy temple.
> Let all the earth keep silent in His
> presence (Hab. 2:20).**

Judah to embrace and believe about their enemies. It is a parody of a funeral dirge. The five woes serve as a tool by which those who are taken captive by Babylon become survivors and not victims—they know the end that is coming for their captors and they understand how depraved cultures lead to downfall. The people of God are to recite them so they might be reminded of God's promise and be transformed from helpless victims to hopeful survivors.

The five woes double as a warning sign of how not to live. The equivalent of a modern political cartoon or caricature, these woes are directed to those who live by something other than faith alone. The righteous live by faith; the wicked will reap what they sow. Babylon becomes an object lesson for what happens to those who overstep the boundaries God has established. When the Babylonians were defeated by the Medes in 539 BC, they were plundered by the nations they had taken captive.

Woe oracles were a common literary form in prophetic writings. They typically contained three elements: a proclamation of suffering, a reason for suffering, and a prediction of doom. This is the pattern we see in the "woe" section of Habakkuk 2. As we read this part of the text, it seems very ancient and irrelevant. The graphic nature and gritty language seem distant and hard to grasp, and the focus on idolatry seems primitive. As we consider the primary social injustices of Habakkuk's day, however, we recognize that they are not so different from those of our modern day. The warnings are directed to a broad, general, and timeless audience, and they are similar to those written by Isaiah (Isa. 5:8–25) and Moses (Deut. 8:12–19).

The word that is translated "woe" to introduce the five catalysts of demise is an onomatopoeic word that was frequently used to introduce a statement of judgment.[1]

⦁ ⦿ ⦿ **GREED**

The first two "woes" relate to extortion and unjust gain. The Babylonians have destroyed people and the earth in their lust for more. In ancient warfare, it was customary to demand exorbitant payoffs in exchange for not leveling a city to the ground. For instance, when the Babylonians conquered Jerusalem, they carried off the treasures of the temple and the palace. They plundered city after city, and the oracle indicates that their debts would be piled up after years of warfare and looting. The original language is graphic; we derive the words for "creditor" and "debtor" from the Hebrew verb meaning "to bite." The prophet warns that the Babylonians have "put the bite on" others for so long that they will be bitten in return.

To the greedy, enough is never enough, and the writer of Ecclesiastes makes that very clear.

> *As the saying goes:*
> Those who love money will never be satisfied with
>   money,
>   and those who love riches will never be happy
>   with what they have. (Eccl. 5:10)

Jesus stated that we would find our hearts where we found our treasure invested, and that's why He talked so much about our money. He was ultimately after our hearts. This is why He praised the generosity of the woman who gave two mites. She gave everything. The way to combat greed is generosity. The more you give away, the less your possessions will possess you. Don't just make a savings plan; make a giving plan.

Ephesians 4:28 tells us there are three ways to gain—stealing it, working for it, or receiving it as a gift. Stealing is rooted in covetousness.

A life of faith means living in such a way that no one is victimized. There is no coveting or getting ahead at someone else's expense. Honesty and integrity are always the right path, and the last of the Ten Commandments addresses this issue: "You shall not covet your neighbor's house; you shall not covet your neighbor's wife, nor his male servant, nor his

> The way to combat greed is generosity. The more you give away, the less your possessions will possess you.

female servant, nor his ox, nor his donkey, nor anything that is your neighbor's" (Ex. 20:17 NKJV).

Bottom line: don't desire what doesn't belong to you. This is the third-longest command, and unlike the other nine, it does not address an outward, discernible, tangible action. Instead, it targets our hearts, deals with our desire, and posts a boundary for our attitudes. It's repeated in the New Testament in Luke 12:15: "Take care, and be on your guard against all covetousness, for one's life does not consist in the abundance of his possessions" (ESV).

This commandment gets at the root of all temptations. If we rewind the story all the way to the beginning, we find that greed was the problem in the garden of Eden. The serpent tempted Eve by planting a seed of suspicion in her mind that God had withheld something important from her. That somehow, she didn't have everything she needed to make her complete. In desperation, she reached out in desire to add something to herself that she thought would fulfill her and make her whole, but the result was the forfeit of the very life for which she was created.

Whenever there is something we want, we should always ask ourselves, "Why?" I've discovered that many things I think I "want" are not even true desires. They are desires that have been warped by greed, covetousness, and pride.

Don't desire what doesn't belong to you.

About ten years ago, I moved back to DC to work as a policy advisor on Capitol Hill, and Pastor Mark asked me if I would come on staff part-time to oversee small groups. We agreed to a deal that included hiring someone full-time in nine months, so I signed up for a nine-month, part-time role to simply tend the groups and encourage the leaders that were already in place. Fast-forward nine months and Pastor Mark asked me to consider coming on staff. I wasn't interested but promised to keep caring for our groups until a suitable replacement was found. For two years, these conversations went on. Finally, in December 2004, I realized my life seemed to be moving toward ministry. So I went into work that day prepared to let my boss know that I would be transitioning out over the next six months or so. I wanted to stay long enough to train someone to replace me, and then I would be moving toward full-time ministry. I strategically thought through my exact words and planned to have the conversation immediately following our Monday morning staff meeting.

The day came, and we all assembled around the conference table to plan for a new week of legislative activity. The moment of my announcement was quickly approaching. At the end of the meeting, my legislative director announced he would be leaving the office in two weeks. The shock of that news made me hit my mental brakes a little bit; my planned departure was in no way related to his departure, and I certainly didn't want it to be construed as such. After the meeting, John followed me into the hall to let me know that he had recommended me as his replacement.

Thanks, God. What do You want me to do now? I didn't know if this was a door or a distraction. The idea of "doors of opportunity" is a popular doctrine in folk theology, but in reality, some opportunities are doors, while others are distractions. I had no idea which this might be. I prayed about it, talked to Ryan about it, and decided I would go through the interview process. I had great respect for the office and for my boss and felt that it was only right that I consider it. In complete fairness to the staff and as a "fleece" before the Lord (see Judges 6:36–40), I also made the decision to be very transparent and forthcoming about my plans. At each stage of the interview process, I represented myself as well as I could, made the most compelling arguments I could make for why I was best for the job, and offered what I believed to be convincing reasons why I was the most qualified candidate. But I also made it very clear that I had planned to leave because I was pretty sure God was calling me into the ministry and I might not accept the job even if it was offered to me. All along, I prayed fervently and genuinely that I would not be offered the job if I was not supposed to take it.

> Folk theology is doctrine we embrace because it sounds comforting or nice but has no footing in Scripture. Stanley Grenz defines it as "a kind of theology that rejects critical reflection and enthusiastically embraces simplistic accep- tance of an informal tradition of beliefs and practices composed mainly of clichés and legends."[2] It's the kind of theology we often wear on our T-shirts and slap on our bumper stickers, such as "God is my copilot," "God will not give you more than you can handle," and "God helps those who help themselves."

What happened? They offered someone else the job. How did I react? Gratitude for answered prayer? Relief that after almost four years the decision had finally been made? Excitement for the next season of my life? Uh . . . NO! I couldn't believe they'd offered someone else the job! I mean, no, I didn't think it was what I was supposed to do; and no, I didn't really want it; and yes, I told them I might not take it even if I was offered the position . . . but what were they *thinking?* Despite the fact that God had answered exactly as

I wanted, my pride still found a way to sneak in and be wounded. I found myself grabbing for something I didn't even want.

Covetousness hits us from all directions. It comes in the form of possessions to be grasped, opportunities to be seized, and relationships to be manipulated. Covetousness fuels more covetousness. The more we give in to it, the more it controls us. The prophet warned that greed will destroy us but God will sustain us. In whatever state of affairs we find ourselves, we recognize God's grace in the midst of it.

UNCONTROLLED APPETITES

My Gran Berry hates watermelons. We call her Gran Berry because her name is Edith Berry, I grew up calling her Gran, and my friends replaced the more formal title of "Mrs." with "Gran" to call her Gran Berry. Gran Berry grew up on a farm,

> Covetousness fuels more covetousness. The more we give in to it, the more it controls us.

and her distaste for watermelons began when she was about ten. It was a season when her uncle Bob had moved into their home and the watermelons were just being harvested from the fields. On the first day of watermelon picking, Uncle Bob cut into a new watermelon every time someone dropped by the house for a visit, and he also cut them for everyone who worked on the farm. Gran thought she should eat a piece every time he cut into a new watermelon. For clarification, a "piece" was anywhere from one-quarter to one-half of a watermelon. People kept coming, Uncle Bob kept cutting, and Gran kept eating. Family legend has held for at least three decades that Gran was trying to show off and impress people with how much watermelon she could eat; she now

> **In whatever state of affairs we find ourselves, we recognize God's grace in the midst of it.**

denies that allegation. Regardless, Gran likely ate a minimum of two whole watermelons that day. Maybe more. It ruined her taste forever, and it was a well-known fact that watermelon was off-limits anytime Gran was around. I once tried to trick her into chewing some watermelon-flavored gum in hopes that I could slowly reverse her aversion, but it didn't work. She claims, "Watermelon looks awful good, but I just can't eat it."

When our appetites are uncontrolled, they eventually destroy us. What once tasted good entices us to destructive behavior, which in turn leaves both us and those in our path in a state of ruin. The Babylonians' appetites were much more extreme and were directed at goals far more devastating than excessive watermelon consumption. The Babylonians were driven by a greed and covetousness that led them on a path of insatiable and damaging desire. Their ambition for more led to violence and their need to dominate compelled them to use alcohol in ways that were detrimental to them and humiliating for their enemies. They inflicted general crimes against humanity and appropriated alcohol to take advantage of, compromise, and eventually humiliate their enemies.

Passion isn't necessarily a bad thing, but when it results in running over others, it has gone too far. Obviously, the Babylonians had a problem with alcohol. We can reach back to verse five of chapter two to discover their susceptibility to its power. Other prophets had warned of its devastating effects on God's own people: "Alcohol and prostitution have robbed my people of their brains" (Hos. 4:11 NLT) The Babylonians would get people drunk and then strip them naked. They also razed the lands that they conquered, stripping them of trees, animals, landscapes, and cities. Nebuchadnezzar cut down all the trees of Lebanon. Psalm 72:16 and Hosea 14:5–7 speak of the lushness of Lebanon. The psalmist had referred to the cedars of Lebanon as the "trees of the LORD" (Ps. 104:16 NIV). Speaking of Babylon's fall, Isaiah 14:8 says, "Even the junipers and the cedars of Lebanon gloat over you and say, 'Now that you have been laid low, no one comes to cut us down'" (NIV; see also Isa. 10:34).

Passion doesn't have to be a negative thing. The Babylonians were intoxicated by their love for themselves and their power, so they executed their strength over others in destructive ways. In Romans 7, Paul wrote of his own struggle with uncontrolled appetites: "*Listen,* I can't explain my actions. Here's why: I am not able to do the things I want; and at the same time, I do the things I despise"

(v. 15). Perhaps that's why he also took great care to remind Christ-followers that we should not be drunk with wine but filled with the fruit of the Spirit: love, joy, peace, patience, kindheartedness, goodness, faithfulness, gentleness, and self-control (Gal. 5:22–23).

Back to Habakkuk, in the middle of this lengthy pronouncement of judgment on those who would pillage and plunder, God pauses to declare that He alone is sovereign over His creation. Regardless of how dominant the Babylonians become, how great their power grows, or how far their empire might extend, God is still omnipresent and omnipotent.

> For as the waters cover the sea,
>> the whole earth will be filled with the
>>> knowledge
> That the Eternal is glorious *and powerful.* (Hab. 2:14)

Habakkuk echoes the words of the prophet Isaiah:

> For as the waters fill the sea,
> The entire earth will be filled with the knowledge of
>> the Eternal. (Isa. 11:9)

While God promised that the earth would be filled with Him, the glory of the Babylonians would slip into the annals of history. God declared, "Now it is your turn! Drink and . . . be exposed!" (Hab. 2:16 NIV). In 539 BC, Belshazzar threw a great party in which the wine flowed freely. That night Darius the Mede captured the city without a fight. The great Babylon fell because of its own uncontrolled appetites. Likewise, unless our passion is in the will of God and for His glory and our craving is for the fruit of the Spirit, we, too, will be destroyed by uncontrolled appetites.

●◦● IDOL FACTORIES

God is still ticked at idolatry.

Those are the words I wrote in the margin of my Bible as I read the Old Testament prophet Jeremiah during Lent. In that moment, I recognized how little time my childhood

> ## The great Babylon fell because of its own uncontrolled appetites.

Sunday school teachers spent telling us stories from that particular book. I never earned a gold star for memorizing Jeremiah 10:5, "Their idols are like scarecrows in a cucumber field" (NRSV). In Jeremiah 50, when a reference is made to "idols" and "images," the original Hebrew phrase is actually "dung pellets." I don't recall any talk of "dung pellets" in my Sunday school class, but that might have made the whole experience more interesting.

The fifth and final "woe" focused on the issue of idolatry. Archaeologists have discovered about fifty pagan temples in Babylon. According to the Greek historian Herodotus, there was a gold statue of Marduk that stood eighteen feet high. While idolatry sounds like an ancient pagan construct that has no bearing on or relevance to our lives today, let us just take a moment to consider what an idol is. An *idol* is anything that takes the place that rightfully belongs to God. It is any-thing that we worship. John Calvin, one of the prominent leaders of the Protestant Reformation, said, "The human heart is an idol factory."[3] We were created to worship, so we *will* worship. We all worship something. We will even create something to worship if we must. We are either worshiping God or we are worshiping an idol, and our hearts are con-stantly shaping and finding idols to worship. Long days of prayer, fasting, and seeking of counsel are not required to expose the idols in my life; they are pretty obvious. They usually surface when I consider the following questions:

- What demands my focus and affections?

- From what do I derive my meaning? To what or whom do I look to tell me who I am and to assign me value?

- Where do I find security, comfort, pleasure, or shelter?

- Whom must I please? Whose opinion counts?

I've always struggled with looking to created things to define me rather than allowing myself to be defined by the Creator Himself. Whether it was a report card, final softball statistics, top billing in the cast of the show, or having the senior engineering design project that was the most inter-esting, I looked to my accomplishments to give me meaning and assign me worth. I sometimes still allow dreams of my own glory to supplant my desire to bring God glory. I have the capacity for some pretty outlandish dreams of glory. When I was six, I dreamed of being the first female in Major League Baseball. In junior high, my goal was to perform on Broadway. In high school, I decided I wanted to work for NASA and eventually become secretary of the interior. By the time I was in college, I had figured out how my life would run to accommodate all of those things. There's nothing wrong with those goals (and I may even secretly hold on to some of them), but I had not given one moment's thought to what any of them had to do with what God might want for my life or how He might desire to get glory out of it. My dreams were focused on making my parents proud and my friends excited, or gaining the attention of those who needed to notice me and recognize my awesomeness. Sometimes my heart's pursuit would be the accomplishment of something that would make the mean kid picking on me sorry for the

> An *idol* is anything that takes the place that rightfully belongs to God.

rest of his life for mistreating a person of my stature. How far I bow down to lesser gods.

Idols may include my career, a relationship, goals, money, success, recreation. It could be my heart's desire for a certain person to accept me or an excessive need for security. We might discover an idol in our lives whenever we say, "I like to think of God as . . ." or when we read something in Scripture that is difficult to swallow and we think, *My God would never . . .* When that happens, it is quite possible we are worshiping a god of our own making and not the God whose name is Jealous.

How faithful am I to God? How much of my focus and affection are centered on Christ? Am I 70 percent faithful to God? Or 90 percent faithful? The scary reality is that 90 percent faithfulness to God is not faithful at all. If we said a man was 90 percent faithful to his wife, we would consider him to be unfaithful. That other 10 percent renders him unfaithful. We can't dabble around with God. We can't just play around with the idea of following Christ. Either He is God and demands all our focus and affections, or He is not and we shouldn't even waste our time. When I consider questions like that, I realize I have bowed my knee to so many things that fall short of God. Idolatry is not relegated to some ancient and pagan culture; it is alive and thriving.

Idolatry happens anytime I think of God as something less than He is. It happens when I knowingly or unknowingly give my attention, love, and focus to something besides Him. Idolatry always enslaves us and exiles us. For instance, when your heart is trapped by pornography, it exiles you from healthy relationships with the opposite sex. If you are married, a gulf is created between you and your spouse because there is a false intimacy you are experiencing with someone else. A lust for power can enslave you and exile you. It's hard to be in healthy relationships with other people if they are the ones you have to climb over to get to the position you want.

Anything we love and trust more than God is an idol that must be ripped from our hearts, and God will tear us away from whatever He must to destroy idols in our lives. While we all come into this world predisposed to being idol worshipers, it's not a lifestyle that we just wake up one day and make a mental decision to live. It's a process that we find ourselves falling into. It's a seduction. Sometimes our idol stems from something bad that happened to us, and we allow that thing to define us and give us meaning. Other times, we start with good intentions—goals, relationships, success—but then we allow those good things to become the center of our focus and affections and they evolve into idols. Often, we don't even realize it.

When I was at Louisiana State University, I spent a lot of time in Tiger Stadium—known as "Death Valley" to many rival schools. Holding ninety-two thousand raving, raging Cajun football fans, the stadium becomes the state's sixth

> **Either He is God and demands all our focus and affections, or He is not and we shouldn't even waste our time.**

largest "city" by population on game day. The roar of the crowd yelling, "Tiger Bait!" to the visiting team can be so deafening that the stadium has been labeled by rival coaches as the loudest and one of the scariest places to play ball. In 1988, the crowd created such a ruckus that an earthquake registered on the seismograph in the geology building.

Decked out in purple and gold, I was like all other good Tiger fans. I rose early in the morning to participate in the weekly ritual of the "tailgate party," where I joined up with friends for good Cajun food, conversation, and games before staking out a prime seat for watching the Golden Band from

Tigerland march ceremoniously into the stadium. Once the game started, I yelled, screamed, jumped up and down, sang the fight song, slapped high fives, and hugged strangers for three hours plus.

But there was one ritual I refused to participate in. At every turnover, the band would play the Chinese Bandits anthem in recognition of the superiority of the LSU defense.

> Anything we love and trust more than God is an idol that must be ripped from our hearts.

The entire student section would then bow down repeatedly in worship of their defensive line. Not me. I refused to engage in any practice that even hinted at worshiping something other than God. I stood there proudly and stoically confident that I would bow down to no idol—not even the LSU football team. Sometimes I felt a little insecure and embarrassed to not be bowing with everyone else. But mostly, I just felt pretty proud of myself. Yet, despite my steeled stance during the football games, I still found myself to be an idol worshipper. I hinged my worth on a professor's opinion. I weighed my value by the opportunities a ministry leader gave me, and I determined my level of spirituality by the number of people who commended my sermon at the campus ministry. I bowed down to people who would value me and opportunities that would promote me. But it was worse than that. Not only did I bow down; I sought people who would bow down to me.

When we look at the idolatrous worship of the Israelites in the Old Testament, they weren't so much replacing God with other gods; rather, they were simply adding to God. An agrarian culture relied heavily on rain and climate, so it was tempting to adopt the agricultural gods of neighboring nations. God's people rarely completely abandoned the one true God; they just wanted to make sure they had their bases covered. We do the same thing. We tend to think in terms of priorities, so we pull out a mental sheet of paper and write "Jesus" at the top. Below it, we list all of the other important people and passions of our lives—family, friends, career, baseball, etc., and we think that makes Jesus "Lord of all." But God doesn't want to be the first in an ever-shifting list of priorities; He wants to be intimately involved with every other priority in our lives. Don't put Him first; put Him central. That will weed out the lesser gods, who promise success and security.

I was an idol worshipper. I *am* an idol worshipper. The final woe to the Babylonians warns me to worship the only One who is worthy of worship.

• ◦ ● BE SILENT; HE IS HERE

God's final words to Habakkuk are found in the abrupt end of the conversation in verse 20:

> But the Eternal One is in His holy temple.
> Let all the earth keep silent in His presence.

That's the last Habakkuk heard from Him. At least it's the last he heard from Him as far as this particular oracle is concerned. God had said, "I am doing a work . . . Wait for it . . . I am seated on the throne."

God had responded to, though not thoroughly answered, all of Habakkuk's questions. The bottom line is, faith will sustain the righteous, the wicked will get what's coming to them, and we can trust this because God is on the throne. In the Hebrew, the word translated "silent" can be pronounced "hush" (*has*). A *hush* will fall over the crowds again in the future, as John recorded, after his vision, that *"a great* silence filled all heaven *penetrating everything* for about half an hour" (Rev. 8:1). When God speaks, there is nothing left for us to do but worship.

At the end of this longest section of the book of Habakkuk, full of judgments and cries of "Woe," God declared that He is on the throne. Thus, Habakkuk came to the end of his questions and complaints to find the presence of God. Just when we think all hope is lost, we discover grace. At the moment we assume God is nowhere to be found, we find Him on the throne. After we have run out of words to complain, question, and plead, we find that silence evokes the greatest answer—an awareness that God is on His throne in His temple.

QUESTIONS

1. Read Habakkuk 2:6–20. What are your initial impressions and reactions?

2. What is the difference between a victim and a survivor? What attitudes and practices differentiate them? What promises of God do you need to hold on to to ensure you are a survivor and not a victim?

3. If your priorities were revealed by your checkbook and credit cards, what would they be?

4. What possessions would you have trouble releasing? Which ones do you think you need to complete you?

5. What appetites need to be controlled in your life?

6. Consider the following questions related to idolatry:

   a. What demands my focus and affections?

   b. From what do I derive my meaning? To what or whom do I look to tell me who I am and to assign me value and worth?

   c. Where do I find security, comfort, pleasure, or shelter?

   d. Whom must I please? Whose opinion counts?

7. Make a list of possessions that possess you, appetites that control you, and idols that give you meaning. Present those to the Lord in prayer and repentance, and ask Him to bring you victory over each one.

8. Take a moment to be silent before the Lord and recognize His presence in your life.

NOTES

CHAPTER EIGHT

ALTARS AT THE INTERSECTION OF WRATH AND GRACE

This is the prayer that Habakkuk the prophet sang to the Eternal One.

I have heard the reports about You,
    and I am in awe when I consider all You have done.
O Eternal One, revive Your work in our lifetime;
    reveal it among us in our times.
As You unleash *Your* wrath, remember *Your* compassion.
    (Hab. 3:1–2)

The final chapter in Habakkuk is a song of praise and has been described as "a message of profound hope in a circumstance of profound despair."[1] It is the explanation of the earlier statement "The just shall live by faith." Curiously, its authenticity has been questioned, and there is some doubt that it was included in the earliest copies of Habakkuk. I learned that as I walked through the Museum of Israeli History in Jerusalem. The Pesher, an ancient commentary found within the Dead Sea Scrolls of the Qumran community, does not

> As You unleash *Your* wrath, remember *Your* compassion (Hab. 3:2).

contain the third chapter, which has led some to suggest that the oldest versions of Habakkuk did not include chapter 3. While this is possible, given the fluid nature of acceptance of Old Testament texts in the first century, it is equally possible if not more likely that the Qumran author simply didn't see any benefit to adding any commentary on this chapter. In other words, the last chapter was likely considered to be less relevant to that community than the rest of the book. Old Testament scholar David W. Baker argues: "Its non-inclusion does not explain its non-existence any more than the omission of many Old Testament passages and books from current preaching proves that they have dropped out of the canon of Scripture."[2] Furthermore, Robert Chisholm draws attention to the idea that the third chapter is a completion of the dialogue patterns and themes as they developed in the first two chapters. That seems to lend support for the third chapter being an original component of the book.[3] The book moves from complaint to confidence, from petition to praise, from doubt to faith. God is still good, sovereign, and faithful, despite the circumstances we see around us, and is therefore worthy to be praised.

Qumran is located about a mile from the Dead Sea and is the archaeological site where the Dead Sea Scrolls were discovered. It is believed to have been the home to the Jewish sect known as the Essenes. The Dead Sea Scrolls contained large portions of the Old Testament, writings from the Second Temple period that were not canonized as part of the Old Testament, and writings related to the rules and community values of specific sectarian groups within Judaism. The Habakkuk Pesher was a commentary used by the Qumran community. We are not sure who wrote it, but it was likely an individual or several individuals within the community.

This great chapter echoes the final chapter of Job and the writings of the psalmists. In fact, Habakkuk uses language that is similar to the Psalms of Trust written by David (Ps. 17) and Moses (Ps. 90). Because the themes are in line with other Old Testament writings, the chapter has survived the test of time and canonization, and it has been proven useful to God's people throughout history, we can trust its significance and message. It is framed as a song for communal singing.

●●● ANOTHER DOOR

"The movie theaters in Union Station are closing next Monday . . ." Pastor Mark continued on with talk of strategizing next steps, notifying leaders, and rolling out the news to the rest of the staff, but my mind was working overtime just to comprehend the first sentence. We had one more weekend of worship gatherings at Union Station.

My story with DC began like most: I came for the politics. Having just completed my master's degree in environmental engineering, I moved to DC to work in environment and energy policy. I was excited and terrified all at the same time, and my first priority was to find a church. Opening the yellow pages (this is a betrayal of my age and not a lack of technological prowess), I made a list of every church that might be a good fit for my one-year adventure on Capitol Hill. One church stood out above all the rest—not because of its size or reputation or denominational affiliation—but because of its location: Union Station. I knew how to drive there, and if I wanted to ensure I would actually get there on time, I could take the Metro. It was an easy first church to visit. I was less sure about the idea of meeting in a movie theater, but I figured that made a first visit even less awkward. If I got there and decided pretty immediately it was not the right church for me, I could just feign an early arrival for the movie. One week later, my list of potential DC churches was obsolete. I had discovered my church home for the next year.

The movie theaters at Union Station were not the first home of National Community Church. That would have been Giddings School. Less than a year into the fledgling church's life, the school was shut down for fire code violations, so a church that barely felt like a church was now a homeless church. Saying "we" came very naturally, even though my history as a member didn't go back that far, because the story of our move from Giddings School to the movie theaters of Union Station was both intimate and legendary. Pastor Mark talked regularly and passionately about the day God shut the door at Giddings School and how that seemed like such a setback in the moment. Nevertheless, he reminded us that if God had not shut that door, we would have never been required to look for another space and we would have never landed in Union Station. From there we

> If God had not shut that door, we would have never been required to look for another....

discovered who God had created us to be—a church living in the middle of the marketplace, believing the church should be the most creative place on the planet, and belonging in the research and development department of the kingdom of God. When we come to a dead end, we must realize that perhaps God just needs to get us to a place where we can look around the corner, make a turn, and step into a greater place of blessing than we would have ever dared to look.

The story was told over and over again, and we all felt we were a part of it. We were grateful that God had closed Giddings School so that we might gather in the movie theaters

of Union Station. We learned that faith was not about con-
juring an idea in our heads and finding ways to fuel it; faith
was recognizing that God always had something better in
mind than what we could see in the present circumstances.
We understood that perspective might not change the facts
of our reality, but they certainly changed our perception of
reality. One seemingly bad day had become a day of destiny for us. As the church grew from 150 to 300 to 750, we

> **Faith was recognizing that God always had something better in mind than what we could see in the present circumstances.**

launched new locations at movie theaters at Metro stops,
and we built our first marketplace environment at Ebenezers
Coffeehouse.

Now, twelve years later, those theaters were closing.
The memories. The convenience. The spiritual birthplace of
so many friends. Once again, we felt a bit like a homeless
church. We still had Ebenezers and our other locations, but
Union Station had been the flagship, the largest location,
and the genesis point. I heard the news on a Tuesday, and
the theaters were closing in less than a week. Our next Sunday would be the first opportunity to share the news with
the congregation and the last time we would gather there.
The next step for me was to contact our small group leaders to let them know the news. I expected disappointment
from those who had invested so many years at the theaters.

I readied myself to walk through some tears from those whose earliest spiritual memories derived from experiences in those movie theaters. It was the place where people had encountered God for the first time, met spouses, dedicated children, made decisions to leave behind perfectly normal and lucrative jobs to depart for the mission field. I prepared myself for devastation and maybe some anger.

The emotions I encountered from our NCC leaders couldn't have been more different. "I can't wait to see what God does next!" "What do you think God might have in store for us?" "I'm so excited about what the next season will bring, and I am so excited to be a part of it!"

What's the difference between people who face the unknown and see fear and those who see opportunity? What makes a person look at a dead end and see open-ended possibilities?

Story. The story we have been told will set the stage for what we expect in the next chapter and will inform us of the role that we play. Mark had told us the story of Giddings School so many times that we just expected the next chapter would be even more exciting. He had recounted to us over and over again the way God works and the character He displays, so we trusted that to be true once again. We knew *who* we were, but more important we knew *whose* we were, and we knew who was writing our story. We knew in our guts that God was sovereign, faithful, and good. We knew that fact intellectually because we had chapter-and-verse support; but we also carried with us the memories of His sovereignty, faithfulness, and goodness in our past. It didn't matter that most of us weren't present for that earliest part of the story; it was still our collective story.

●◦● THE STORY

The Bible is a collection of sixty-six books and letters that tell one seamless true story. It includes all the elements of good storytelling: heroes, villains, murder, mystery, intrigue, passion, suspense, nobility, betrayal, and sacrificial love. But

> What's the difference between people who face the unknown and see fear and those who see opportunity?

we must be careful to remember that it is not just a good story; it is a true story and it is *the* story that gives life, meaning, and perspective to all of our stories.

In this last chapter of Habakkuk, the prophet declared, "I have heard the reports about You, and I am in awe when I consider all You have done" (3:2). In the midst of prayers gone wild, Babylonian threats, and a lengthy discourse of woes, Habakkuk found hope in the stories he had heard of God's power, providence, sovereignty, goodness, faithfulness, and mercy. Throughout Scripture, God continually reminds His people of His Story and their story. The book of Deuteronomy was given to the children of Israel near the end of their wanderings in the wilderness. In many ways, it is a rewrite of the Law in Exodus, Leviticus, and Numbers, but the tone is different. Deuteronomy is a message of remembrance and hope to a new generation, who did not experience the early miracles of the liberation from Egypt; Moses wrote to remind them of who they were, whose they were, where they were going, why they were going there, and how they were to live once they arrived. He told them to remember the commands of the Lord, repeat them to children, recite them when at home and away, make them the last topic of conversation at night and the first topic of conversation in the morning. He said, "Do whatever it takes to remember them."

There are several moments where Scripture itself or one of its characters will hit the pause button to remind people of their story. At the end of Joshua's life, he recounted the story for those newly settled in the promised land to remind them of God's favor and blessing during their wilderness wanderings. First and 2 Chronicles are basically a rewrite of 2 Samuel, 1 Kings, and 2 Kings, and are believed to have been written for a postexilic audience as they returned to their promised land. The author may have intended to chronicle the rise and fall of the people of God so they could live in His blessing and avoid future calamity. God even instructed the people to celebrate feasts and erect monuments so the story could be passed from generation to generation. As Stephen stood on trial before the Sanhedrin, he told the story of God's work among Israel as his defense (Acts 7).

> The Sanhedrin was the ruling body for the Jews during the time of Christ. It was led by the high priest and had civil, criminal, and religious jurisdiction.

In the book of Judges, we observe a vicious cycle: "Another generation grew up who did not acknowledge the LORD or remember the mighty things he had done for Israel" (Judges 2:10 NLT). They had forgotten the works and ways of God.

When Habakkuk came to a place where God's actions collided with his expectations, he found the only hopeful response was worship that was rooted in an unshakable and undeniable awareness of God's character, ways, and works. The same is true for us, and we grow in our awareness of His character as we grow in our understanding of His Story and as we embrace that story as our own.

● ● ● KNOW GOD'S STORY

Most of us read our Bibles a little bit like we read our yearbooks. Maybe I was just a particularly narcissistic student, but I didn't read the yearbook cover to cover. In fact, there were certain pages I never even explored. Whenever I got a new yearbook, I immediately turned to the pages where I could find pictures of myself and pictures of my friends. The Chess Team page had nothing to offer me because I was not there.

We read the Bible the same way.

We enjoy the stories from the book of Genesis because they seem familiar to us. We turn to Psalms and Proverbs because they contain so many truth bombs that we are certain to find something there to keep us afloat for one more day. The New Testament offers us many easy application points. We love the stories and the Gospels and the epistles because we "find" ourselves there. David, Joshua, and even Peter all make sense to us. However, for all the stories where David kills the giant and Joshua marches into Jericho, there are also the stories where the Babylonians conquer and Moses is left to die in the wilderness. Furthermore, we tend to ignore Leviticus and Judges and the

> We can and should see ourselves in the Bible, but the main character is God Himself.

Prophets because it's harder to see ourselves there and the text doesn't immediately apply to us. The problem with that approach is that we are left with only a partial view of the story, and we fail to recognize that the story is not first and foremost about us. Certainly, we can and should see ourselves in the Bible, but the main character is God Himself. When we put the spotlight on God and keep Him center stage, all the random stuff begins to make a little more sense and we have a broader perspective on the stories that He is writing in our own lives. That means we have to turn to the places that are a bit harder to grasp than the ones we find comforting and inspirational during our fifteen-minute morning devotional time.

Stop reading the Bible like a yearbook and start reading it like the autobiography of God. Then, you begin to see threads of His character, ways, and purposes. Themes of redemption run through every moment of wrath, and promises of justice frame every pronouncement of judgment. That's when the Bible ceases simply to be snapshots of disconnected stories or self-help for the day and starts to be a framework upon which we can hang our whole lives.

● ● ● KNOW GOD'S STORY IN HISTORY

Most of us read the Bible because we know it's an important spiritual discipline. Many of us also recognize it's important to know the story of God in our own lives; we often call this our "testimony." Meanwhile, we tend to forget that God has been at work for two thousand years since the close of the canon of Scripture and before our arrival on the scene. The subject of "church history" may sound

> Promises of justice frame every pronouncement of judgment.

like a snoozer, but what if we remember it is the story of God that has been marching on ever since the last pages of Scripture were written? As Bruce Shelley says in *Church History in Plain Language*, "Many Christians today suffer from historical amnesia,"[4] and that amnesia has crippled our faith and our knowledge of God's character. Church history is more than an intellectual study of dates and dead people; it is the record of God's continued faithfulness and goodness to His people. When we study it, we can see more clearly the redemptive threads in our own lives. Even in its darkest days and most tenuous moments, the church has survived persecution, heresy, inquisition, crusades, and, some might argue, Christian television. She has persevered through the insecurities, pride, false motives, and failures of those who have claimed to love her and to lead the bride of Christ. Our collective history serves as a reminder of the beauty of our faith—that it isn't up to us. It's all about God, His grace, and His sovereignty.

Reading biographies about the faith of martyrs or the resolve of missionaries or the determination of reformers can fuel our faith and spark renewed hope in the midst of circumstances we face, redirecting our focus to the Author who never puts down the pen.

KNOW GOD'S STORY IN OUR LIVES

Knowing God's story in our own lives requires us to look for it, mark it, and commemorate it. In 1803, Congress appropriated twenty-five hundred dollars for the exploration of the Louisiana Purchase. That expedition was led by Meriwether Lewis and William Clark. Today, we have thousands of pages of journals kept by the men on that journey. We know that on Thursday, May 31, 1804, "several *rats* of Considerable Size was Caught in the woods to day."[5] On January 27,

1805, Clark wrote that "Lewis took off the Toes of one foot of the Boy who got frost bit Some time ago."[6] Every ship contains a logbook with details on where the ship has been and what it has encountered. Journaling does three things: it helps us mark and measure movement, it helps us remember where God has brought us, and it helps us see more of His works and ways.

When I was in engineering school, I was forced to draw everything in my notebook—specimens, lab equipment, experimental setups, etc. Whatever I saw under the microscope, I had to sketch it, and I absolutely hated it. I don't have an artistic bone in my body, and I found the practice embarrassing and useless. Until exam time rolled around. That's when I appreciated all those drawing assignments. I recognized that because I was forced to draw, I was forced to look more carefully. Drawing the specimen helped me see it better. Colors, textures, shapes, and distinguishable patterns didn't always emerge on my first look or second look, but as I looked again and again, new information was stored in my memory and new categories were created for remembering it. I think the same thing happens when we journal. As we see God more, we are able to praise Him more. We more clearly recognize and acknowledge the hand of God at work in our lives, and the practice becomes an act of worship and a hymnal for worship in days to come.

There are many kinds of journals. In Scripture, we find that the Psalms are basically praise and prayers captured from the journals of people like Moses, Asaph, and David. Lamentations is a journal containing Jeremiah's reflections on the fall of Jerusalem. Ecclesiastes was Solomon's journal as he reflected on life and its meaning. I've kept prayer journals so I can remember to thank God when He answers them; I've kept sermon journals to remind myself of teachings that may be meaningful down the road; I've kept devotional journals to record the insights God gives me as I read the Bible. One of the best journals I have ever kept was a gratitude journal. At the end of each day, I recorded three things for which I was particularly grateful that day. Sometimes it was a particular conversation or event that was meaningful. Often, it was the name of a person. Other times, it was as mundane as "thank you for the bed that I am lying on right

> As we see God more, we are able to praise Him more.

now. A lot of people don't have a bed or a roof over their heads, and I don't want to take that for granted."

There is another practice in Scripture that reminded the people of their movement and God's role—the making of altars. Abraham, Isaac, Jacob, Moses, Gideon, and Samuel all built altars and monuments to remember a moment of God's provision and faithfulness or to mark a significant conversation or interaction with Him. In Joshua 4, we find the Israelites standing on the banks of the Jordan River, gazing across their first barrier to the promised land. At Joshua's command, the priests stepped into the river with the ark of the covenant, and the waters separated for the people to cross on dry land. After they had crossed, Joshua sent representatives from the twelve tribes back to set up memorial stones in the river. Joshua told them, "Someday when your children ask you, 'Why are these stones piled up here?' you will tell them how the waters of the Jordan parted as the covenant chest of the Eternal One crossed the river, and these stones will fix that memory for the Israelites forever" (Josh. 4:6–7).

> Set up markers along the road; put up guideposts *so you can find your way home* (Jer. 31:21).

As the people of God were being captured and deported by the Babylonians, the prophet wrote God's instructions: "Set up markers along the road; put up guideposts *so you can find your way home*" (Jer. 31:21). Sometimes we need some signs and symbols to remember where we have been and where we are going. There may even be physical places of spiritual significance to which we can make pilgrimage. In the book *Draw the Circle*, Mark Batterson explains, "Going back to places of spiritual significance can help us find our way forward again."[7]

Journaling doesn't have to be a discipline of writing in a locked book that we keep under our pillows, and altar making doesn't require us to be stonemasons. Not all of us are writers or artists. The point is to devise a systematic plan for marking and measuring our movement and God's work in our lives. It could be a Twitter feed or a Facebook page. It could be a photo book or a photo stream that captures the faithfulness of God. Maybe it's a collection of stones from significant places in your life. I've started keeping a list of "altar moments" on my phone to recall the moments when God showed up in my life in undeniable and unmistakable ways. It's always with me to be edited or reviewed. We need to find ways to capture our story and remember God's work in a way that broadens our view and shifts our perspective. Journaling helps us see more of God's hand, which enables us to worship Him more. Like Habakkuk, we can remember God's works and worship Him for His ways, so that we can return to a place of awestruck wonder at His character.

WRATH AND MERCY

Habakkuk includes an interesting request: "As You unleash *Your* wrath, remember *Your* compassion" (3:2). The NIV simply states, "In wrath remember mercy." Habakkuk acknowledges an attribute of God that we like to ignore—wrath—and then juxtaposes its activity with that of another attribute we love—mercy. Surprisingly, God never seems to shy away from the topic of His wrath. Perhaps even more surprisingly, these seemingly opposite dimensions of His character often show up together. For instance, the first display of God's wrath in Scripture is found in Genesis 3, when He kills one of His creation to make clothing to cover the nakedness of Adam and Eve. Interestingly, His wrath was also the first display of personal grace and mercy to Adam and Eve; it was wrath that activated grace. We see wrath and mercy showing up in other places, as well. From the sparing of Rahab on the walls of Jericho to the redemption of Isaac on Mount Moriah, God's mercy always shows up with His wrath. Sometimes it seems as though His wrath activates His mercy, sometimes it seems as though His mercy activates His wrath, and other times He shows mercy in the midst of His wrath.

The cross is the most poignant example of God's wrath and mercy intersecting. As God poured out His wrath on

> **God's wrath is inseparable from His love, His goodness, and His holiness.**

His Son hanging on the cross, He activated grace and mercy on our behalf. In other words, His wrath made salvation possible for us. God's wrath is inseparable from His love, His goodness, and His holiness; it activates His grace for our good, and reflects His glory. Like Habakkuk, we can acknowledge the fullness of His character—not separating His qualities into good traits and bad traits but viewing them as inseparable components of grace.

Habakkuk then begins to recount specific examples of mighty acts of grace in the story of the people of God. The technical term is "theophany." While there is much speculation regarding the specific events he was referring to, they all point to moments in history when God displayed His goodness and faithfulness, such as the deliverance of Israel from Egypt, His guidance of their conquest of Canaan, and His victory over the Philistines. Habakkuk seems to point to historical figures like Othniel and Gideon. Elements from the song of Deborah (Judg. 5), the songs of Moses and Miriam (Ex. 15, Deut. 32), the wilderness wanderings (Ex. 16–17, Num. 21–25), and Psalms (68, 95, 107, 136) seem to be included. D. Martyn Lloyd-Jones said, "The God in whom I believe is the God who could and *did* divide the Red Sea and the Jordan River. In reminding himself and us of these things, Habakkuk is not just comforting himself by playing with ideas; he is speaking of the things that God has *actually done*. The Christian faith is solidly based upon facts, not ideas. And if the facts recorded in the Bible are not true, then I have no hope or comfort. For we are not saved by ideas; but by facts, by events."[8]

Habakkuk remembered God's presence, His acts of deliverance, and His displays of power. Each stanza is separated by a pause . . . indicated in the Hebrew by the word *selah*. The meaning of the word is somewhat unclear, but it most likely means to pause for a breath and functions in biblical songs as a musical divider.[9] It calls attention to what has been said, and Habakkuk is the only place it shows up in Scripture outside the Psalms. It's also likely that each of the three stanzas was followed by the refrain, "LORD, I have heard of your fame; I stand in awe of your deeds, LORD. Repeat them in our day, in our time make them known; in wrath remember mercy" (Hab. 3:1–2 NIV).

James Bruckner, editor of *The NIV Application Commentary* for Habakkuk, helps us understand the structure in which it might have been sung:[10]

- Stanza 1: Title: Habakkuk 3:3a
- Pause

- Stanza 1: Habakkuk 3:3b–8

- Refrain

- Stanza 2: Title: Habakkuk 3:9a

- Pause

- Stanza 2: Habakkuk 3:9b–13a

- Refrain

- Stanza 3 Title: Habakkuk 3:13b

- Pause

- Stanza 3: Habakkuk 3:14–15

J. Vernon McGee observed that the book of Habakkuk "begins with a question mark and ends with an exclamation point."[11] He stands before God and declares, "I stand in awe of your deeds . . . repeat them in our day" (v. 2 NIV). We echo that prayer every time we pray, "Your kingdom come, Your will be done."

QUESTIONS

1. Read Habakkuk 3:1–16. What do you learn of God's character and Habakkuk's character from this passage?

2. Habakkuk claimed to be in "awe" as he considered what the Lord had done. When was the last time you were in "awe" at the Lord's work in your life?

3. Read Joshua 24:1–18. What do we learn about God's ways and His works from this passage? In verse 16, the Israelites responded that nothing could be farther from their minds than abandoning God, yet we see in Judges

that they abandoned Him only one generation later. What happened? How can we avoid the same mistake?

4. Read Acts 7:1–50. What do we learn about God's character from this passage?

5. Make a list of some of the moments where God revealed Himself to you in ways that were undeniable and unmistakable. Name a time when God proved His:

   a. Goodness

   b. Faithfulness

   c. Sovereignty

   d. Mercy

   e. Power

   f. Compassion

   g. Wrath

6. What are some practical ways that you can begin marking, measuring, and remembering God's work in your life? How can you help others recognize God's presence and celebrate it with them?

7. God's wrath and mercy often show up together in Scripture. Can you think of some other examples?

8. This week, incorporate Habakkuk 3 into your personal worship time. Write down your own version of it and pray it each day.

NOTES

CHAPTER NINE

THE LAND OF "IF NOT"

Even if the fig tree does not blossom
>and there are no grapes on the vines,
If the olive trees fail to give fruit
>and the fields produce no food,
If the flocks die *far* from the fold
>and there are no cattle in the stalls;
Then I will *still* rejoice in the Eternal!
>I will rejoice in the God who saves me!
The Eternal Lord is my strength!
>He has made my feet like the feet of a deer;
He allows me to walk on high places.

For the worship leader—a *song* accompanied by
>strings. (Hab. 3:17–19)

FAITH FOR FURNACES

The Bible is replete with parables and promises that are predicated with the word "if." Consider the cause-effect chain reaction that is ignited if we believe, if we pray, if we have faith, if we open our Bibles to

- 2 Chronicles 7:14: "If my people, who are called by my name, will humble themselves and pray and seek my face and turn from their wicked ways, then I will hear from heaven, and I will forgive their sin and will heal their land." (NIV)

- 1 John 1:9: "If we confess our sins, he is faithful and just and will forgive us our sins and purify us from all unrighteousness." (NIV)

- Matthew 17:20: "If you have faith as small as a mustard seed, you can say to this mountain, 'Move from here to there,' and it will move. Nothing will be impossible for you." (NIV)

- Matthew 21:22: "If you believe, you will receive whatever you ask for in prayer." (NIV)

- Revelation 3:20: "Here I am! I stand at the door and knock. If anyone hears my voice and opens the door, I will come in and eat with that person, and they with me." (NIV)

God's character is revealed to us and His blessings are discovered when we dare to step out on faith in the "if." Throughout Scripture, we find people on the brink of desperation who were willing to embrace the potential found in that simple proposition. Like the synagogue official and the unclean woman, many in Scripture dared to believe in the possibility that "if" we act in faith or "if" God shows up, the possibilities are endless.

But what happens if . . . not? What if you are humble, pray, seek, and turn, but your nation still moves toward ruin? What if you muster all the faith you can but it still doesn't seem to equate to a mustard seed? What if you believe the character and promises of God and are faithful to do what comes after the "if" but God doesn't pull through on His end?

God's answer to Habakkuk's prayer came in a succession of attacks from the Babylonian armies of King Nebuchadnezzar. In 605 BC, Babylon invaded and deported select

> God's character is revealed to us and His blessings are discovered when we dare to step out on faith.

young Jewish men with great potential to be trained in Babylonian culture, language, and literature. Four of those men were Daniel, Hananiah, Mishael, and Azariah. We know the latter three better by their Babylonian names: Shadrach, Meshach, and Abed-nego.

When given food and wine from the king's table, these four young men refused to eat it, likely because it did not comply with Jewish dietary laws and/or it had been offered as sacrifices to foreign gods. Their commitment to the one true God was so strong that we read in Daniel 1:8 that

Daniel "resolved that he would not defile himself with the king's food, or with the wine that he drank" (ESV). After proposing an alternative plan of eating fruits, vegetables, and water, the four young men were tested, examined, and

> ## What if you muster all the faith you can but it still doesn't seem to equate to a mustard seed?

found to be better nourished than the youths who ate the king's food. Not only were they healthier, but when they stood before the king, he found them to be ten times better than all of his court magicians, and they were elevated to positions of influence in the king's palace.

Two years later, the king had a dream that troubled him, and no one could tell him the meaning of it. Enter Daniel. With the help of God and the prayers of his three friends, he was able to accurately relay the details of the dream and provide the interpretation. Nebuchadnezzar praised the God of Daniel and promoted Daniel to be chief prefect over the wise men of Babylon. At Daniel's request, his three friends were promoted, as well, and Nebuchadnezzar praised the God of Daniel and his friends.

Many years later, Nebuchadnezzar constructed an idol—ninety feet high and nine feet wide—and he called all of the leaders and government officials of the empire to come to its dedication. Government leaders and those in positions of power were directed to worship the idol. The ancient commentator Jerome said, "It is the higher ranks which stand in the greater peril, and those who occupy the loftier position are the more sudden in their fall."[1]

Nebuchadnezzar instructed the crowd: "When the musicians begin to play you must fall down and worship. If you do not fall down and worship, you will be thrown into the fiery furnace." Three men refused to bow down: Shadrach, Meshach, and Abed-nego. The king flew into a rage and summoned them.

"*It is reported to me* that you, Shadrach, Meshach, and Abed-nego, refuse to serve my gods and do not *bow and* worship the golden statue I had set up. Is that true? If you are ready to *comply with my order and* fall down and worship the statue I have made when you hear the sound of the horn, flute, lyre, lute, harp, pipe, and all the other musical instruments, then things will go well for you from here. But if you refuse to worship, you will be taken immediately and thrown in a furnace of blazing fire. What god could possibly rescue you from my hands then?" (Dan. 3:14–15)

Check out their courageous response in Daniel 3:16–18: "Nebuchadnezzar, we have no need to defend our actions in this matter. *We are ready for the test.* If you throw us into the blazing furnace, then the God we serve is able to rescue us from a furnace of blazing fire and release us from your power, Your Majesty. But even if He does not, O king, you can be sure that we *still* will not serve your gods and we will not worship the golden statue you erected."

This brand of faith knows God can . . . believes He will . . . but worships even if He doesn't. These men's faith sent the enemy into such a fit of anger that his face distorted with rage.

We don't need to defend ourselves, and we don't need to defend God. If you throw us in, God is able to deliver. But even if He does not . . .

But even if He doesn't. It's the declaration of "if not" faith. The first "if" statement was rooted in God's ability.

> This brand of faith knows God can . . . believes He will . . . but worships even if He doesn't.

This second "if" statement has nothing to do with His ability but everything to do with our response to His perfect, sovereign, mysterious will.

In that moment, Daniel's friends did not know the outcome. They clung to the promise that God can *and* acknowledged the reality that He might not. Though their circumstances might change, God's character would not. They stood precariously in the land between if and if not. They stood strong in "He is able" confidence and "if not" faith while recognizing that a furnace stood between those two worlds.

Once again, there are two ways we can look at God and our circumstances. We can frame the character of God according to our circumstances, or we can frame our circumstances according to what we know of the character of God. We can let our circumstances inform what we know to be true of God or we can let what we know to be true about God inform our circumstances. As Warren Wiersbe said, "God doesn't always change the circumstances, but He can change us to meet the circumstances. That's what it means to live by faith."[2] These three men allowed God's character to frame their circumstances. They recognized that when God is in the equation, all bets are off. When God is involved, we step into the land of infinite possibilities. In desperate situations that called for decisive courage, they clung to the knowledge that God would deliver them if He so desired.

It is entirely possible that God's words through the prophet Isaiah were echoing in their heads and stirring hope in their hearts:

> **Eternal One:** When you face *stormy* seas I will be
> there with you *with endurance and calm*;
> you will not be engulfed in *raging* rivers.
> If *it seems like* you're walking through fire with
> flames *licking at your limbs*,
> *keep going*; you won't be burned. (Isa. 43:2)

Many heroes of the Bible had "if not" faith. Moses never made it to the promised land; Hosea married a prostitute who ran away; and Paul probably took that thorn in his flesh to the grave. Habakkuk declared his faith in the land of "if not," and it inspires us to stand strong, as well.

WHEN "IF NOT" HITS HOME

I preached on "if not" faith one Sunday morning at 9:00, and by 3:00 p.m. that day, I was on a flight to Nashville, Tennessee, accompanied by my teammate Emily. I rarely travel alone because traveling is such a great opportunity for discipleship and accountability, and it's just a lot more fun. On the plane, I asked Emily, "Where is the place where you are having to embrace 'if not' faith right now?" She had listened to the message three times that weekend. She's also my sermon-writing buddy, which means she had endured countless hours reading the text with me, listening to me

> Habakkuk declared his faith in the land of "if not," and it inspires us to stand strong, as well.

verbally process how to make it relevant, and helping me craft my words. She responded, "None. All I could think about when I sat through every service was all of the 'if nots' that other people close to me were facing. I can't think of any that I'm walking through right now."

Twelve hours later, Emily and I had separated ways for our own meetings, but I got a phone call from her. With a shaky voice, she asked, "Can you pray for my sister? She's been admitted to the hospital and they are running tests."

I responded out of appropriate obligatory concern more than genuine compassion: "Do you need to go home?"

"No, just pray."

Thirty minutes later, I was in the car, heading to a conference and a board meeting, when Emily called again. This time, she was clearly emotional. "My brother-in-law just called. The baby needs to come today." The words should have been filled with excitement, but I could tell that the tears were not those of joy. Still unaware of the severity of the situation, I decided to stop off at the Starbucks to see her before going to my meeting. When she said, "They don't think my sister is going to make it," it finally hit me: *This is serious. And I'm skipping the conference.* We got in the car and hit the interstate for West Virginia. We drove for seven hours in quiet dread and desperate prayer.

Emily's sister had been diagnosed with eclampsia and was facing the delicate balance of life and death for both mother and baby. The baby was not ready to come, but the fluid around the baby was becoming toxic to the mother. To delay birth would be dangerous to Emily's sister. To speed up the birth would endanger the baby. And in the midst of that tension, seizure threatened both mother and child.

We found ourselves in the land of "If Not." All of a sudden, the story of three Jewish men facing a furnace and the principles I had outlined in my message the day before became very tangible and raw. All of my sermon points that were so easy to preach behind the security of my pastoral role and pulpit became real-life tests. What kind of faith were we going to have?

We watched blood test results, ate fast food, and moved from hotel to hotel as rooms in the uncharacteristically busy town of Charleston, West Virginia became available. We prayed. We cried. We believed, and asked God to help us in our disbelief.

•◦◉ NO FOOD ON THE TABLE

Habakkuk ended his book with one of the most beautiful and poignant passages in all of Scripture, and he wrote it from the land of If Not. As his song comes to a conclusion, its tone and form change. In musical terms, it would be called a "bridge." The previous sixteen verses declare the

> He declared his faith even when there was no visible sign of God's presence.

visible proofs of God's sovereignty, goodness, and faithfulness. In his conclusion, he declared his faith even when there was no visible sign of God's presence. He sang of joy even when the most obvious sign of God's presence—food on the table—was not there. He stared into the probability of empty fig trees, barren olive trees and vines, and pasturelands littered with cattle carcasses, and declared that God is strength and salvation. To fully grasp the impact of these statements, it's important to remember that the economy of Judah was based on its agriculture. Farmers and shepherds were the major players in ancient commerce. Habakkuk thus proceeded to mention every possible source of food and agricultural business in the ancient world: fruit, wine, olives, field crops, cattle, and sheep. There would be nothing to eat, drink, or wear.

Such devastation should not have come as a shock since Moses had declared centuries before that failed crops and

faltering livestock would be the ramifications for unfaithful-
ness to God's covenant (see Deuteronomy 28:15–24). In Jeremiah we see the Babylonian invasion and the description of
exactly what Habakkuk had seen:

> **Eternal One:** They will devour your harvest and
> your food.
> They will devour your sons and daughters.
> They will devour your *livestock,* flocks, and herds.
> They will devour your vineyards and orchards.
> (Jer. 5:17)

Even when our livelihood is destroyed, God is strong.
Even when all hope is lost, God is salvation. Stripped of
everything, the prophet recognized the presence of his Creator, Redeemer, and Sovereign Lord was all he needed. There
is an intimacy reflected in his words as he declares God to
be "my" strength. Habakkuk lived by the kind of faith God
described in verse 4 of the previous chapter. It's a faith that
stands strong when God's actions don't seem to match His
character and promises as our finite minds perceive them.
His conclusion sounds similar to many of the songs of praise
and worship we find in the Psalms. However, the Psalms
tend to praise God for His provision and protection, while
Habakkuk praises God in the absence of provision and
protection.

DELIVERANCE FROM, THROUGH, AND LATER

Remember, it's about trusting God's purposes. Romans 8:28
states, "And we know that God causes everything to work
together for the good of those who love God and are called

according to his purpose for them" (NLT). We are reminded that God calls not according to gifts, abilities, vision, great ideas, or education. He calls according to *His purpose*. He works things together for His purpose and not our expectations, and His purpose is always tied to His character and sovereignty.

Sometimes God delivers *from*. Noah and his family lived

> ## He works things together for His purpose and not our expectations.

safely inside the boat, completely dry, as the floodwaters covered the earth. A ram was provided in the thicket as a replacement for Isaac. Jonah was spit out of the giant fish. Peter escaped from prison. I love it when God delivers from.

Many times, God delivers *through*. Daniel had to go into the lion's den. Shadrach, Meshach, and Abed-nego had to walk through the fire. Jesus had to go to the cross. We love the unexpected twists in the stories when God delivers through. This is the way God delivered my friend Mardie. Through the meticulous skill of doctors and the prayers of passionate intercessors, God delivered Mardie through the valley of the shadow of death, and she delivered a healthy and determined little preemie named Lyla Claire. I'm so grateful for the times that God delivers through.

Sometimes, however, God delivers *later*. The saints in Hebrews 11:35–40 did not receive all that God promised. They put their hope in life postresurrection. In his second letter to the Corinthians, Paul reported that he was plagued by some sort of "thorn" in his flesh (12:7). We don't know what it was—it may have been a sickness, an addiction, a physical deformity. I think it was probably Peter. He asked God three times to remove it. The answer: "My grace is all you need. My power works best in weakness" (v. 9 NLT).

Whether He delivers from, delivers through, or delivers later, we know that He is always present *with*. Psalm 139 says we can't escape His presence. When the psalmist walked through the valley of the shadow of death, God did not promise deliverance; He promised presence (Psalm 23). "I am with you." It's one of the most abundant and hopeful promises of the Bible. There are purposes to be discovered in His presence regardless of the circumstances.

"If not" faith means submitting to God's purposes, knowing they are rooted in His character.

STRENGTH

The central declaration in the song in Habakkuk 3 is "The Eternal Lord is my strength!" (v. 19). Other translations have rendered it "The Sovereign LORD is my strength" (NLT). This statement is common throughout Scripture:

When Saul sent men to kill David, the psalmist sang, "I will *lift my voice to* sing Your praise, O my Strength" (Ps. 59:17).

Emerging victorious through the Red Sea, Moses and Miriam praised God: "The Eternal is my strength and my song" (Ex. 15:2).

Considering the destruction that had come to Israel, Isaiah declared, "For the Eternal, indeed, the Eternal is my strength and my song" (Isa. 12:2).

Branded a traitor, and weeping over the horror of the Babylonian invasion, Jeremiah professed, "O Eternal One, You are my strength" (Jer. 16:19).

The word translated "strength" in these verses is the Hebrew *oz*,[3] but that word is absent from Habakkuk's song.

> **Whether He delivers from, delivers through, or delivers later, we know that He is always present.**

For his profession of "if not" faith, Habakkuk used the word *hayil*, which we translate "strength," but it could also be understood as "army." In other words, for Habakkuk, God was his army. His faith was not rooted in what he could see but in what he could not see in the moment. He anchored into the brand of faith that the author of Hebrews described: "Faith is the assurance of things you have hoped for, the absolute conviction that there are realities you've never seen" (11:1).

In turn, God gave not just stamina but vitality. Habakkuk would not simply endure the hardship that was to come; rather, he would thrive in the midst of it, walking like a deer on the heights. He echoed the psalmist once again:

> The True God who encircled me with strength
> and made my pathway straight[,]
> He made me sure-footed as a deer
> and placed me high up where I am safe.
> (Ps. 18:32–33)

Habakkuk began in chapter 1 staring up at an insurmountable problem and ended in chapter 3 on top of the mountain. What do we do in the land of "if not"? How do we respond when we know God can, believe He will, but realize He may not? Habakkuk sang, and the song was meant to be sung by the entire population of Judah. In fact, according to the directions included at the end, it is likely that the song was used in temple prayers accompanied by musical instruments. It is not enough for us to worship God individually; our faith is sustained and increased as we worship Him within the context of community. Our faith may be personal, but it is never private.

Webster's Dictionary lists "noun" as the primary part of speech for the word *worship*, but for the follower of Jesus, *worship* should primarily be a verb. In particular, *worship* is listed as a "transitive" verb. My mom was an English teacher for many years, so I know full well that a transitive verb requires an object. *Worship* is a transitive verb, and the critical component is its direct object—God.

When we worship God, it causes our strength to increase.

●◎◉ ETERNAL OUTLOOK

The brand of faith I live with most often is furnace-avoidance faith. I am not willing to go into the very place where God gets the most glory.

When Jesus told the disciples they had to eat His flesh and drink His blood, the crowds disappeared. The disciples remained. They didn't have anywhere else to go. They weren't keen on becoming Cannibals for Christ. But at the same time, they had passed the point of no return. They had believed too much and invested too much. Sometimes, leaving Jesus takes more faith and energy than remaining. We don't really want to stay with Him, but it's just more trouble to leave Him.

Early Christianity was accused of being "cannibalistic" because of the ritual of the Eucharist, also called communion or the Lord's Supper. Reports spread that the followers of Christ were "eating His body and drinking His blood," and the practice was misunderstood as literal. The early Christians were also thought to be incestuous because they married people to whom they also ascribed the familial titles of "brother" and "sister."

Habakkuk says, "The Sovereign Lord is our strength." Sovereignty means that God is in charge. Eternally in charge. We need God to redefine our suffering against the background of eternity because eternity puts things into perspective. Theologian Alister McGrath said, "If the Christian hope of heaven is an illusion, based upon lies, then it must be abandoned as misleading and deceitful. But if it is true, it must be embraced and allowed to transfigure our entire understanding of the place of suffering in life."[4]

Every now and then God will give us some grace moments during our grief. Not always but sometimes. My granddaddy passed away a few years ago, and when I heard the news, the first thing I heard God whisper to me was, *"You'll see him soon."* I guess I could have interpreted that message as an ominous prediction of imminent demise, but when I heard God speak that to me in that inaudible but powerful way

> We need God to redefine our suffering against the backdrop of eternity because eternity puts things into perspective.

that He speaks to us, I had a "knowing" deep in my gut—my granddaddy is exactly where he lived to be, and in the grand scheme of the timeline of eternity, I'm going to see him soon.

As we gaze through the lens of our lives, we need to adjust the aperture so that eternity comes into focus and redefines everything else in the picture. In Romans 8:18, Paul said, "I consider that our present sufferings are not worth comparing with the glory that will be revealed in us" (NIV). This is coming from the man who according to 2 Corinthians faced prison, five floggings, shipwreck, snakebites, hunger, thirst, and cold for the sake of the gospel. "You see," he said, "the short-lived pains of this life are creating for us an eternal glory that does not compare to anything we know here. So we do not set our sights on the things we can see *with our eyes.* All of that is fleeting; *it will eventually fade away.* Instead, we focus on the things we cannot see, which live on and on" (2 Cor. 4:17–18).

I need to be more like Shadrach, Meshach, and Abed-nego and exchange furnace-avoidance faith for the kind of faith that is willing to go wherever God gets the most glory. I long to be more like Habakkuk and declare God's character boldly in the land of "if nots." I don't know why some stories end well and others do not. I don't know why Marva lost her life while Lyla Claire was born healthy and happy. I can't reconcile why God would intervene to erase someone's headache but not heal Brian's leg. Why did Shadrach, Meschach, and Abed-nego emerge from the fire while a few hundred years later thousands of devoted followers of Christ would burn at the stake?

I refuse to let what I don't know keep me from worshiping what I do know.

O. Palmer Robertson poetically summarizes the hope of Habakkuk, "Songs in the night anticipate the glad arrival of the eternal dawn in which the faithful shall receive their ultimate vindication."[5]

QUESTIONS

1. Read Habakkuk 3:17–19. In what circumstances would Habakkuk continue to worship God?

2. Read 2 Corinthians 11:23–27. In what circumstances did Paul continue to serve God?

3. Read Daniel 3:16. What would you have done if you were in the same position as Shadrach, Meshach, and Abednego? What tests threaten to compromise your faith?

4. Do you tend to view God's character through the frame of your circumstances? Or do you tend to view your circumstances through the frame of God's character? Do you allow your circumstances to define God's character, or do you let His character define your circumstances?

5. According to which aspects of God's character do you need to frame your current circumstances?

6. Sometimes God delivers from, sometimes He delivers through, and other times He delivers later. What are some examples of each from Scripture, your own life, and the lives of those around you? Why do you think He would deliver different people in different ways? Are those reasons important for us to know?

7. Read Isaiah 40:28–31. Memorize it.

8. Use Habakkuk 3:17–19 in your personal worship time this week.

NOTES

CHAPTER TEN

BACK TO THE PIT

Sometimes we fall into pits. The reason could be because we were careless, ignored warning signs, or walked through the caution tape of God's boundaries. Other times, we fall in through no fault of our own; life just dumps us there. Some are pits of suffering—health deteriorates, marriages disintegrate, children wander, and careers end. Other pits are just frustrating—someone else gets the promotion, every investment we make goes belly up, our new workout adds ten new pounds. I've found that there are times when I can handle the "big stuff" better than the little stuff. When tragedy strikes my life, I can recognize it as an opportunity to "believe God for a miracle." It's almost as though I can taste a bit of the glory of the martyr. It's the little stuff that reveals just how little I really trust God's character. It's the careless tweet from someone I've never met who thinks he or she has the right to comment on a shirt I wore to preach in two years ago that sends me into that place of committing murder in my heart. It's the little stuff that sneaks into the cracks in our hearts that open them for us to see just how wounded, untrusting, fearful, and angry they are.

I emerged from my pit in the sidewalk in the rain. In fact, I emerged relatively unscathed, but my leather briefcase and heels never recovered. My physical condition was intact, but I felt really dumb. Sometimes we feel the worst about ourselves because of what life drops on us (or drops us into) as opposed to what we do to ourselves. The short story is that a guy eventually walked up and helped me get out. Okay, I didn't do anything at all. The ground was so unstable that there was absolutely nothing I could do to get out without making the situation worse. I literally just reached up, relaxed, and let him pull me out (although not before he asked me how much I weighed). It's a rather anticlimactic end to an otherwise thrilling story. The police cars, flares, and caution tape showed up a few hours after I rose out of the pit and walked home quietly muddy. The incident taught me a few things. One, life drops you to places of desperation through no fault of your own. Two, sometimes you need the help of someone bigger, stronger, and with different perspective. And three, you have to trust that person's perspective and yield to his or her help.

THE REST OF THE STORY

In the first part of the book, we told the Story of God up to the part when the Babylonians were breathing down the necks of the people of Judah. Habakkuk cried out to God "Why?" and "How long?" and God answered in a way he did not expect. Everything God said came true. The Babylonians sent the people of Judah into exile for seventy years. The story didn't end there, however. God's people returned to their land, and great leaders like Ezra and Nehemiah made a valiant effort to lead them back to worship.

Their efforts failed. The prophets were no more. The pen of the Author stopped writing. For four hundred years the people of God waited on the stage of history in darkness. And the curtain seemed to close on God's Story.

Those in darkness waited silently . . . hopefully . . . for God to speak again.

Then an angel showed up to a Jewish teenager named Mary and announced that she would be the mother of

> Those in darkness waited silently . . .
> hopefully . . . for God to speak again.

the Messiah. God split the timeline of human history in two. And in a stone feeding trough made for animals, God pierced through the darkness with the sound of an infant's cry. Wrapped in the skin of His own creation, subjected to the care of His own creation, God invaded the reality of human history with one objective: to rescue His children from the hands of the villain, so that at the name of Christ, every knee would bow and every tongue confess that Jesus is Lord, to the glory of God the Father.

He turned water into wine and showed mercy to sexually promiscuous women and healed the sick and commanded dead men to walk out of their graves and showed honor to the scum of society. He preached love and offered peace. But the villain twisted people's hearts, even entering into the heart of one of Jesus' own followers, who ultimately betrayed Him into the hands of those who would kill Him. He was mocked, spit upon, beaten, and forced to carry a wooden beam on His back up Skull Hill, to a place where nails were driven into His wrists and feet and a crown

> **God invaded the reality of human history with one objective: to rescue His children.**

of thorns was pressed into His skull. And there . . . on a cross . . . Jesus died.

Darkness covered the earth. Jesus' body was placed in a borrowed tomb. All seemed lost. All hope was gone. But this time, the curtain did not fall but was ripped in two. The Author kept writing. The Story was not over. For the tree that Jesus hung His life on became for us a tree of life.

On the day after Sabbath, the stone rolled away and the Messiah walked out of the tomb, conquering sin and death, crushing the villain's head, and offering us life.

He commissioned His followers to spread His story to the entire world and promised to send them the Comforter in His place. The disciples returned to Jerusalem to pray and wait.

The Holy Spirit blew upon the believers on the day of Pentecost, and three thousand people were added to the church in one day (Acts 2). They faced tension and problems and hostility. They were imprisoned and persecuted. The disciples preached—in homes, on the streets, in prisons. The gospel spread throughout the Mediterranean world. Peter, John, and Paul pleaded with the churches to maintain good doctrine, to hold fast to the Word of God, to plant their lives firmly in the Story He was telling. The great preachers of the first century were beheaded, crucified, and tortured to death because they refused to turn away from the words of this book. They knew their objective—to tell the story of Jesus to the world so His name might be praised. And they were willing to face any obstacle to make it happen. For them, to live was Christ. To die was gain. And the Story of God exploded across the globe.

• ◎ ● REDEFINITION

We understand and experience salvation at a much deeper level than Habakkuk was ever able to because we live on the other side of the cross, where our salvation was purchased by Christ. It should give some assurance to know that, as Christ hung on the cross, He faced suffering that goes beyond what any of us could imagine. Hanging on the cross, Jesus Christ, fully God and yet fully man, cried out, "My God, My God, why have You forsaken Me?" (Matt. 27:46).

The writer of Hebrews expands on Jesus' suffering for us: "For Jesus is not some high priest who has no sympathy for our weaknesses *and flaws*. He has already been tested in every way that we are tested; but He emerged victorious, without failing God (Heb. 4:15).

Just as Habakkuk said he would worship "if not," Jesus said, "Not My will . . ." (Matt. 26:39).

"So let us step boldly to the throne of grace, where we can find mercy and grace to help when we need it most" (Heb. 4:16).

We can run the race that God has set before us by keeping our eyes focused on Jesus, on whom our faith depends

> We can run the race that God has set before us by keeping our eyes focused on Jesus.

from start to finish. He was willing to die a shameful death on the cross because of the joy He knew He would experience after, and that's the adventure He has called us to follow.

We may never understand our circumstances. We may have trouble seeing God at all in the midst of them. But we can allow Him to redefine them. Redefinition is not an immediate process. It may take years. I can't redefine your situation for you and your friends cannot redefine it for you. Only God can redefine it for you when your circumstances seem to contradict His character and promise. In those moments when we are at a loss for how to respond, the response of this one man Habakkuk might be helpful. We can go to that lonely place where all hope seems lost and God seems distant, but hold on tight to the parts of His character that still make sense—the grace moments He's given us in the past, an identification with the sufferings of

Christ, the promise of eternity. We can declare His goodness, affirm our joy in our salvation, and proclaim our hope in eternity.

QUESTIONS

1. What are the "pits of desperation" in your life right now? Do you feel that you have fallen in through your own fault, or do you feel circumstances just conspired against you? Does this change how you handle your problem?

2. How easy do you find it to ask for help? To receive it? Have you ever been in the position of being actually helpless and having to relax and let someone else rescue you?

3. Do you think God wants us to try to get out of the pit, or to call for help? What makes you think so?

4. What would getting out of the pit of desperation look like to you? How do you think this might fit in with God's long-term plans for you?

5. What does it mean to "live on the other side of the cross"? How is your perspective different from Habakkuk's?

6. Read Hebrews 4:15–16. How does this relate to you?

7. Are you allowing God to redefine your circumstances? What might this look like to you in your life right now? How can you more fully allow this to happen?

NOTES

NOTES

CHAPTER 1: THE STORY

1. O. Palmer Robertson, *The New International Commentary on the Old Testament: The Books of Nahum, Habakkuk, and Zephaniah* (Grand Rapids: Eerdmans, 1990), 1.

2. Gordon Fee, *Reading the Bible for All Its Worth* (Grand Rapids: Eerdmans, 2003), 181.

3. Robert B. Chisholm, *Handbook on the Prophets* (Grand Rapids: Baker Academic, 2002), 9.

4. *The Princess Bride*, directed by Rob Reiner (1983), motion picture.

5. Gordon Fee, *Reading the Bible for All Its Worth*, 182.

6. Chisholm, *Handbook on the Prophets*, 433–34.

7. Robertson, *The New International Commentary on the Old Testament*, 136.

8. Ibid., 37

CHAPTER 2: FALLING

1. O. Palmer Robertson, *The New International Commentary on the Old Testament: The Books of Nahum, Habakkuk, and Zephaniah* (Grand Rapids: Eerdmans, 1990), 135.

CHAPTER 3: PRAYERS GONE WILD

1. Richard D. Patterson, *Wycliffe Exegetical Commentary: Nahum, Habakkuk, Zephaniah* (Chicago: Moody, 1991), 175.

CHAPTER 4: GOING THE DISTANCE

1. J. I. Packer, *Concise Theology* (Wheaton, IL: Tyndale House, 1993), 56.

2. James Bruckner, *The NIV Application Commentary: Jonah, Nahum, Habakkuk, Zephaniah* (Grand Rapids: Zondervan, 2004), 214–15.

3. John Patrick Shanley, *Doubt* (New York: Theatre Communications Group, 2008), 6.

4. Warren Wiersbe, *Be Amazed* (Colorado Springs: Victor, 2004), 139.

5. Bruckner, *The NIV Application Commentary*, 215.

CHAPTER 5: WRITE IT DOWN

1. Stephen R. Miller, *Holman Old Testament Commentary: Nahum, Habakkuk, Zephaniah, Haggai, Zechariah, Malachi,* ed. Max Anders (Nashville: Broadman & Holman, 2004), 62.

2. Henry Cloud, *When Your World Makes No Sense: 4 Critical Decisions That Can Bring Hope and Direction into Your Life* (Nashville: Thomas Nelson, 1990), 38.

3. Michael Ireland (Worklife.org), "'Experiencing God' Author Sees Hope for Revival," website of Blackaby Ministries International, accessed August 20, 2013, http://www.blackaby.net/expgod/2010/12/03/experiencing-god-author-sees-hope-for-revival/.

CHAPTER 6: LIVING FAITH

1. S. M. Lehrman, "Habakkuk," in *The Twelve Prophets,* Soncino Books of the Bible, ed. by A. Cohen (London: Soncino, 1948), 219.

2. John Calvin, *Commentaries on the Twelve Minor Prophets,* in O. Palmer Robertson, *The New International Commentary on the Old Testament: The Books of Nahum, Habakkuk, and Zephaniah* (Grand Rapids: Eerdmans, 1990), 181.

3. James Bruckner, *The NIV Application Commentary: Jonah, Nahum, Habakkuk, Zephaniah* (Grand Rapids: Zondervan, 2004), 236.

4. Ibid., 236–37.

5. Warren Wiersbe, *Be Amazed* (Colorado Springs: Victor, 2004), 107.

6. Stephen R. Miller, *Holman Old Testament Commentary: Nahum, Habakkuk, Zephaniah, Haggai, Zechariah, Malachi,* ed. Max Anders (Nashville: Broadman & Holman, 2004), 52.

7. Alberto Ferreiro, *Ancient Christian Commentary on the Old Testament: The Twelve Prophets* (Downers Grove, IL: InterVarsity Press), 190.

CHAPTER 7: WOES

1. O. Palmer Robertson, *The New International Commentary on the Old Testament: The Books of Nahum, Habakkuk, and Zephaniah* (Grand Rapids: Eerdmans, 1990), 189.

2. Stanley J. Grenz and Roger E. Olson, *Who Needs Theology? An Invitation to the Study of God* (Downers Grove, IL: InterVarsity Press, 1996), 27.

3. *Institutes of the Christian Religion*, bk. 1, chap. 11.8 in John Calvin, *Institutes of the Christian Religion*, rev. ed., trans. Henry Beveridge [n.p.: Hendrickson, 2008], 54–55, paraphrased.

CHAPTER 8: ALTARS AT THE INTERSECTION OF WRATH AND GRACE

1. Walter Brueggemann, *An Introduction to the Old Testament* (Louisville: Westminster/John Knox, 2003), 244.

2. David W. Baker, *Tyndale Old Testament Commentaries: Nahum, Habakkuk, and Zephaniah* (Downers Grove, IL: IVP Academic, 1988), 45.

3. Robert B. Chisholm, *Handbook on the Prophets* (Grand Rapids: Baker Academic, 2002), 434.

4. Bruce L. Shelley, *Church History in Plain Language* (Nashville: Thomas Nelson, 2008), xv.

5. Meriwether Lewis and William Clark, *The Journals of Lewis and Clark*, ed. Bernard DeVuto (New York: Houghton Mifflin, 1981), 6.

6. Ibid., 78.

7. Mark Batterson, *Draw the Circle* (Grand Rapids: Zondervan, 2012), 214.

8. D. Martyn Lloyd-Jones, *From Fear to Faith: Studies in the Book of Habakkuk and the Problem of History* (London: Intervarsity, 1953), 71.

9. Stephen R. Miller, *Holman Old Testament Commentary: Nahum, Habakkuk, Zephaniah, Haggai, Zechariah, Malachi*, ed. Max Anders (Nashville: Broadman & Holman, 2004), 80.

10. James Bruckner, *The NIV Application Commentary: Jonah, Nahum, Habakkuk, Zephaniah* (Grand Rapids: Zondervan, 2004), 252.

11. J. Vernon McGee, *Thru the Bible Commentary Series: Nahum and Habakkuk* (Nashville: Thomas Nelson, 1991), 65.

CHAPTER 9: THE LAND OF "IF NOT"

1. "St. Jerome, Commentary on Daniel (1958). pp. 15–157," trans. Gleason L. Archer, http://www.tertullian.org/fathers/jerome_daniel_02_text.htm, accessed May 31, 2013.

2. Warren Wiersbe, *Be Amazed* (Colorado Springs: Victor, 2004), 136.

3. "5797. oz," from *Strong's Concordance*, Bible Hub, http://biblesuite.com/hebrew/5797.htm, accessed August 21, 2013.

4. Alister McGrath, *Intellectuals Don't Need God and Other Modern Myths: Building Bridges to Faith Through Apologetics*, (Grand Rapids: Zondervan, 1993), 108.

5. O. Palmer Robertson, *The New International Commentary on the Old Testament: The Books of Nahum, Habakkuk, and Zephaniah* (Grand Rapids: Eerdmans, 1990), 248.

ABOUT THE AUTHOR

A native Alabamian, Heather Zempel currently leads the discipleship efforts at National Community Church in Washington, DC, where she oversees small groups, develops leadership training, and serves on the weekend teaching team.

Heather followed a circuitous route into full-time ministry. Having obtained bachelor's and master's degrees in biological engineering from Louisiana State University (Geaux Tigers!), she worked as an environmental engineer and as a policy consultant on energy and environment in the United States Senate before coming on staff at National Community Church. Heather is passionate about exposing emerging generations to the mystery, drama, and comedy of the biblical text and inspiring them to explore it for themselves.

Heather lives on Capitol Hill where she can be found enjoying theater with her husband Ryan, searching out the best barbeque joints, and nerding out on church history. She is also the author of *Sacred Roads* and *Community is Messy*, and you can read about her ramblings on small group environments, discipling the next generation, and SEC football at www.heatherzempel.com.